Priceless ♡ Inspirations

Priceless Inspirations

Antonia "Toya" Carter

FP

Farrah Gray
Publishing

www.fgpbooks.com

Publisher: Farrah Gray Publishing
          P.O. Box 33355
          Las Vegas, NV 89133

Credits:
Editorial: Karyn Langhorne Folan
          Dr. Marcia Brevard Wynn
Cover Shot: Reggie Anderson
Cover Design: Dontay Barnes

Priceless Contents♡

1. HOUSE AND HOME

2. BOYS TO MEN

3. SEX AND LOVE

4. PREGNANCY AND MOTHERHOOD

5. HEARTBREAK AND HEALING

6. DRUGS AND ALCOHOL

7. DOMESTIC VIOLENCE

8. MONEY AND FAME

9. FRIENDS AND USERS

10. GOSSIP AND THE TRUTH

11. SELF ESTEEM AND BODY IMAGE

12. TRUST AND REAL LOVE

Foreword

Toya…One amazing woman, super mother, defiant leader, and awesome friend. She's a cup full of love. Toya is drawn to every aspect of life. She is helpful and forgiving. Toya wears her intentions on her heart, therefore, she loves all. Because her strength is love, she's stronger than the mind can imagine.

I can honestly say she's my 1st love and I support this book 100 percent…Toya Good Luck!

~Lil Wayne

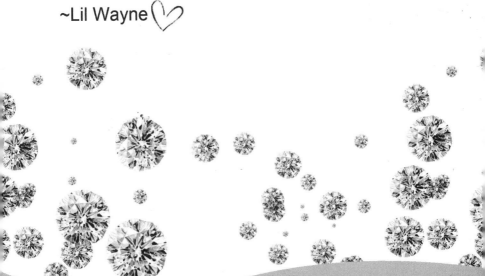

Introduction

It's been said that "everything happens for a reason." I don't know who said it first, but I believe it. If God brings you to it, He'll bring you through it, for reasons we don't understand most of the time.

While I was going through some of the things that have happened in my life, I didn't understand them at all. Why didn't I have a home? Why didn't I have loving parents? Why was I always so alone? Was there something wrong with me? Was it something I did? These questions were constantly in my head, and I couldn't understand my situation. My parents didn't know it at the time they gave me my name, but I found out not too long ago that "Antonia" means "priceless" in Italian. It's funny. Most of my life, I didn't feel "priceless." In fact, I felt just the opposite.

I felt like a rolling stone most of the time, rolling from one relative to another and from home to home, beginning at the age of 12. I'd stay a few months here or there, and then it was on to the next home. I was always bouncing from one place to the next, sleeping on couches and in spare rooms. I was constantly struggling at school, at home, with my family members and in my relationships. It felt like my situation would never, ever change. I was always looking for guidance, usually taking it from the wrong people and finding myself in deeper than I had been before. I was always looking for love. Sometimes I found it, but most of the time I didn't. I learned a lot, most of it the hard way.

I'm still learning, but I understand things so much better now than I did as a scared, pregnant, 14 year old girl, who had no money, no help and no idea how to be a mother. I remember writing all my thoughts and feelings down in a notebook, and when I read those words now, the emotions come back to me like I am going through everything again for the first time. I want to share some of my experiences with you in this book, just so you know my story. Things might look good for me now, but not too long ago, everything in my life was all messed up. *I* was all messed up.

There are so many young girls and women out there who are struggling, looking for guidance, and looking for someone who understands what they're going through. I've read their letters, their emails, their tweets and their Facebook messages. They've seen me on *Tiny and Toya* and they reach out, even though we don't really know each other. There is a connection because they know I can relate. They've seen the issues I'm dealing with on the show trying to raise my daughter, my relationships with men, my mother's struggle with her addiction and how it impacts me and my life. They know I've been through some of the same stuff they have, and that I've managed to come out on the other side. Sometimes smiling, sometimes with tears in my eyes, but I've survived and I've kept moving forward. I've tried to not let the past make me bitter, but better. I've tried to keep my heart open. I've tried to walk with faith in God and the hope that the future might be better. I may be bent, but I'm not broken, and I don't want you to be broken either.

Sometimes, I wish I could talk to my younger self. I would teach the girl I used to be some of the things I know now and save

her the pain of making the mistakes I have made. I know that I can't. What I *can* do is reach out to other young girls and young women out there. I can reach out and say, "I've been where you are. Don't give up." I can reach out and say, "I've been where you are. Don't make the mistakes I've made." I can say, "Hold on, little sister. Dig deep into your faith in God and in yourself and stay strong because you can make things better."

I'm writing this book to you, and in a way to my younger self, too, because all the hurts and struggles of my life have taught me some things. I hope the things that I have learned can help someone else. I hope the things that I have learned can help *you*. Unlike some books that try to skip over the heavy parts and make it seem like life is one big, happy, fairy tale, I'm gonna keep it really, really, real. I'm gonna lay it out there, both the good and the bad. Being fake is not my style. I've never been that way. I'm not pretending to be an expert and I'm not a doctor. I'm just a person who has made mis takes and learned from them, and who is not afraid to say so.

This is my story, both my mistakes and my victories.

In every chapter, I try to address something that's really going on for young women and girls, everything from family drama, to love and sex, motherhood, domestic violence, and even the drama that some of us go through with the people who are supposed to be our friends.

If telling my story helps even one young girl, then it'll be more than worth the pain of remembering some of my darkest moments. It might even be the reason God led me to those dark places in the first place.

Love,

Toya

House And Home♡

Antonia "Toya" Carter

House And Home

I spent a lot of my life looking for the place where I belonged. I spent a lot of my life looking for my "home."

I know a lot of young girls and women feel like they don't have anybody, and like they don't belong anywhere. Maybe it's because there's a lot of drama in their home life and they're constantly scared and worried about what might happen next. Or maybe they're like I was and they don't feel like they have the love of their parents. Maybe they're bouncing from place to place, from pillar to post, never feeling wanted, and it makes them angry. Some girls grow up without a roof over their heads at all. They live in shelters, in foster homes, or even on the streets.

Do you feel me? Does this sound like you? It was me when I was coming up. It was me for a long, long time. When you don't feel like you've got someone in your life who really loves you, everything is harder. I know firsthand. Everything was harder for me because I was always looking for love.

When you don't feel like there's anyone in your life who wants to take care of you, you grow up feeling alone. Again, I know this personally. I felt alone many times in my life and it made me so angry and so sad that I didn't know what to do, other than lash out.

When you don't feel like you have anyone in your life that will always be there for you, it gets real hard to believe in yourself. I didn't believe in myself for the longest time. I felt like I didn't have anything special or anything unique. I made all kinds of mistakes, looking for a place where I belonged and felt wanted.

Eventually, I found my way, but the process was hard.

Antonia "Toya" Carter

Sometimes I made it even harder than it should have been because I was always chasing the wrong things. Chasing my idea of what a "home" should be led me away from family members who loved me and into the arms of boys who didn't. This ultimately led me into single motherhood. This also got me into fights, put me in some dangerous situations and made me a grown woman before I was out of high school.

I learned some priceless gems about life along the way that I hope will encourage you if you're feeling unwanted and alone. I hope my story will keep you from making the same mistakes I did.

"She ain't nothing but a crack whore."

"She oughta be ashamed."

"She ain't never gonna get herself together."

They knew I was listening. They *wanted* me to hear it. Sometimes they even tossed their comments in my direction, saying stuff like, "You probably gonna be just like her."

I was about ten years old, and at this point in my life, I barely knew my mother. I only saw her when she came to visit me at my Uncle Frank's house, maybe once a month or so, but I still didn't like the way the family talked about her. What kid wants to hear their mom talked about like that? No kid wants to hear words like that about their mom, and I was no exception.

It made me angry to hear them running her down like that in front of me. It made me want to know for myself what kind of woman my mother was. I think I wanted to prove them wrong somehow. The truth was, though, at that point in my life, I didn't know anything much about her other than what her own family said about her.

I didn't even live in the same house with her, and by this time, I had begun to wonder why. As a young girl, I couldn't remember a time when I had lived with my family at all. I'd always lived on the other side of town with my great uncle, Frank, and then when he died, with my great aunt, Edwina. My brothers were with our mother and father. Why wasn't I? My cousins lived with their mothers and fathers. Why didn't I? Didn't they want me? Was there something wrong with me? I looked at the families of some of my friends and saw them living with their parents, or at least one of their parents. Why was I different?

Instead, there I was, living with Aunt Edwina in the house she had shared with my Uncle Frank until he'd died a few years before. There I was, growing up with cousins who were a lot older than me, when I had brothers around my age in the same city. There I was, sleeping in a room in my aunt's house that had once been the dining room, but had been converted to a bedroom, while my mother lived in the 7th Ward in the Marabou Apartments, without me.

"Crackhead."

My aunt spit out the words and looked at me. She was my mother's sister, but that didn't stop her. She seemed to be enjoying it. I felt like she was going out of her way to call my mother out of her name in front of me. It was like she knew that by calling my mother names, she was calling me names, too.

Was it my fault that my mother had a drug problem? I

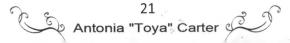

didn't know.

My aunt kept talking. Every now and then, her mother, my grandmother, would tell her to cut it out.

"Stop talking that way," she'd say in a low voice, jerking her head in my direction.

"I don't care!" My aunt's voice got louder. "If she don't know, she needs to know!"

Listening to my aunt talk, I felt all kinds of emotions. I felt confused about why I didn't live with my mother and angry at her for the things her own family said about her. I felt curious about whether the rumors and gossip were true, and unsure about whether she loved me. Most of the time, I didn't say these things out loud to anyone. Sometimes, though, my feelings bubbled over and spilled out. I lashed out and I fought back. Once, I even struck out at that mean old aunt with her hard words. I wrote about it in my journal:

> I can't believe her! What kinda aunt is she to talk that way about her own sister? As soon as I got into Grandma's house, she started talking about my mama. She didn't even want to let me in the house at first. Tried to stand at the door and block me. But it's Grandma's house and she couldn't stop me. So then she started with her mouth: "Your mama was here with her crackhead self. Nerve of her, bringing that stuff here to my mama's house. She need to quit running the street and come and get y'all asses."
>
> She went on and on, running down Mama in front of me

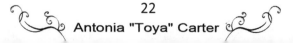

and I got sick and tired of it. I just decided I was gonna make her shut her damn mouth and if she didn't want to shut it, I was gonna shut it for her.

"Stop calling my mama a 'crackhead'!" I screamed in her face. "Stop it!"

"Little girl, you need to shut up or I'll whip your ass." She got this real serious look on her face and I knew she was gonna hit me in a minute, but I didn't care. I don't back down from a challenge from nobody and she's old, too. I probably coulda made her swallow her teeth.

"Come whip me then," I shouted. "Come whip me, if you can, I don't care. You ain't no kinda aunt anyway! Don't you get it? She still my mother and I love her, so don't be calling her out of her name in front of me!"

"I call her a crackhead because that's what she is!"

I went at her, swinging for all I was worth. I wanted to hurt her—I wanted to hurt her so bad. I would have ripped every hair out of her head if I could have.

My grandmother stepped into it and pulled me off of her. She told me how wrong I was and tried to make me apologize, but I wouldn't. And I won't. I won't do it. I hate her. I hate her and I always will.

Now, I understand that fighting my aunt was really, really

disrespectful and I'm embarrassed that I did it. At the time, I had so many feelings of hurt, confusion and shame, and I kept them bottled up inside me. The only thing I could let out was the anger. It was the only emotion I felt safe with, and it grew and grew the older I got, the worse my mother got and the more I needed her.

By the time I swung on my aunt, I knew that a lot of what she was saying was true, but when I first started visiting my mother at her apartment in East New Orleans, I didn't know for sure. At the time, I was only ten years old. It would be years later before I tried to press her for answers, and even now, I hold back. As a kid, I didn't even know how to ask what I wanted to know. I knew I couldn't walk up to her ask, "Are you a crackhead?"

Some of the earliest memories I have of trying to get to know my mother at that age was of sitting in her dark apartment, feeling bored.

Taken Away

The story they had told me up to that point in my life was that my Uncle Frank said, "I'm going to get that little baby. That baby girl is too pretty to stay up in there."

Uncle Frank's children were all nearly grown. His youngest was in high school, and his wife was a stay-at-home mother who loved the idea of raising another little girl.

He just went and got me. That was the reason I lived with Uncle Frank and his family, or so I thought for the longest time. It wasn't until years and years later that I asked my parents about why I never lived with them, and why they let someone take me and never tried to get me back.

When I heard the answers, they nearly broke my heart. The truth was, at that time, my parents loved drugs more. They just did, and that was all there was to it. So when you say you feel like "nobody cares about you," I can relate. When I was a baby, my parents basically gave me away.

Uncle Frank was an older man. He was my grandmother's brother. I know lots of people are raised by their grandmothers. You might wonder why my grandmother's brother came for me, and why my grandmother didn't. I've often wondered, too. For some reason my grandmother and I just aren't close. I'm not sure why. There's probably a reason, some family problem or secret that I am not aware of. There was a time when I felt hurt by it. I couldn't understand why all of my mother's family seemed to hate me, why they had so many negative things to say about me, and why my pictures were never on the mantle at my grandmother's house, but I don't care anymore. It's all right. Uncle Frank and his wife, my Aunt Edwina, were good to me. They gave me my first real home and they protected me.

I don't remember my parents visiting me there, but much later on, they both told me that they did. They said they came and wanted to take me places with them, but I hid my shoes so I wouldn't have to go. They said I cried.

I guess even then I knew that things weren't "all good" with either one of them. Or maybe, to my toddler eyes, they were strangers. Aunt Edwina and Uncle Frank were the only "parents"

I'd known, even if I didn't call them "Mama" and "Daddy." Besides, why would I want to leave? I was happy living with them.

Later, when I was older, I'd learn how heavily addicted my mother had become by that point. She was running the streets with the worst of characters trying to get drugs. I learned about the things she'd do, and let others do to her, just to get enough money to get high.

I learned these things later. As a very little girl, all I knew was I lived with Uncle Frank and Aunt Edwina and that everything was happy and good for me at their house. That is until Uncle Frank passed away when I was six.

I was there when it happened. He was lying on the couch and me and one of my cousins were playing with him. Playing with Uncle Frank was an almost every day thing at their house. Uncle Frank would come home from his job and sit on the couch and we'd be all over him, rubbing his head and wrestling and stuff. He never seemed to mind. Usually he'd be laughing and trying to tickle us and everyone would be acting silly and having fun. But on this day, after just a little playing, he rolled off the couch and hit the floor. At first we thought he was just playing around, even though he hit his head pretty hard when he fell. We jumped on him, rolling around on top of him, laughing and tickling.

But he wasn't playing. He was having a stroke, and we didn't know it.

When he stopped moving and his face sort of froze in

this expression that wasn't normal, we finally realized this wasn't a game. One of my cousins called the ambulance. I'll never forget when the paramedics came and strapped him onto their gurney and took him out of the house. I remember feeling very scared.

I never saw him alive again.

I don't remember anything about his funeral, or anything much about the days after that, but I'll never forget Uncle Frank. He taught me a lot about how a real man takes care of his family. He taught me what family life looks like. He taught me about love.

I spent years after he passed away trying to get that life back.

After Uncle Frank's passing, I stayed with Aunt Edwina. By now, my four cousins, her children, had grown up and moved out, so it was just me and her most of the time. She was an older lady by now, old enough to be my grandmother, but she still had enough energy and love to care for me.

Uncle Frank's death was hard on her. By the time I was nine or ten, I knew that Aunt Edwina drank too much in the years after Uncle Frank's death. Sometimes when she was drinking, she was hard to be around. She wasn't mean or abusive, but it was like she'd get lost in her own feelings and forget I was there. If home is really where the heart is, her home and her heart were broken after losing Uncle Frank. I was young, but I kinda understood. I tried to get out of her way and let her grieve. At the same time, I was becoming more curious about my own family.

Around that time, my father went to prison. A lot of my mother's family was talking about him and my mother. I was getting older, old enough to listen in on the things adults whispered to each other. Then they stopped whispering and spoke plainly, to my face.

My mother's family didn't think much good about her or my father, and they let me know they didn't think much of me either.

"You're gonna be just like her, ain't you?" My aunt rolled her eyes at me when she said it and looked disgusted. "Ain't you?" How could I know the answer? I didn't even know my mother, and I realized I had to find out about her.

From Crack House to Crack House

Mom lived too far from Aunt Edwina's house for me to walk, so I had to get someone to take me over there when I wanted to go. I pestered my cousins and older relatives. They knew that Aunt Edwina wasn't in the best of health and I guess they hoped that seeing me might help my mother, too. So they took me.

I don't remember what I expected to happen when she saw me. All I can tell you is that it wasn't like a happy TV reunion where the mother and the daughter fall into each other's arms crying.

I don't remember her being glad to see me. Maybe she was, but she didn't seem to know how to show it. I don't think she even hugged me or kissed me or anything. She didn't play with me, but we talked a little. She didn't ask me how I was doing in school, or what kinds of things I liked to do.

She never took me anywhere to show me off, but sometimes we would go upstairs to visit "the candy lady", a lady who sold little two cent candies to the children in the building. She never said "I love you" but she would tell me I was pretty and ask to brush my hair. She didn't ask me to come back and live with her.

It would be like, "Oh. Hi, Toya," and then she'd go back to whatever she was doing. She was in her own world. Now that I'm older, I understand that she wanted her kids and that she loved us, but she couldn't reach us from where she was.

I don't remember feeling disappointed, but I know her attitude had an effect on me. I'd gone to her looking for some kind of connection, but I didn't feel it. I didn't feel anything. My father was away, in jail, and not expected back for a year. I ended up sitting in her front room and watching television with my brothers and playing games.

I started visiting her every couple of weeks or so. The more I visited, the more I noticed that there were always a lot of people coming and going at her house. It hurt me so bad to have to admit that the negative things her sisters said about her might be for real, but I couldn't deny it, sitting there, watching shady people come in, stay a few minutes, then leave. At least I didn't see her get high or anything like that. She didn't do any of that in front of me on those visits.

My brothers weren't so lucky. My older brother, Walter,

and my younger brother, Josh, had stayed with her when Uncle Frank came for me. They saw much more of the awfulness of her addiction than I ever did. They raised themselves. As for the houses, as time went by and she spiraled deeper and deeper into her addiction, the places they lived got shabbier and shabbier. Later, when I was in middle school and high school, I can remember passing by a home and hearing people say the place was a "crack house" with the same disgust I'd heard in my aunts' voices. I was too ashamed to tell them that my mother and brothers *lived* there.

By then, I didn't want a home with her. I was embarrassed by her. I wanted to pretend like I didn't know anything about her. Feeling shame about your people makes you feel even more alone, especially if, deep down inside, you wonder if it's true that no matter how hard you try, you'll end up just like them. Especially if everywhere you look, it seems like all your friends and their mothers have beautiful, perfect relationships, and your mother doesn't seem to know that you're alive.

What a Mother-Daughter Relationship Was Supposed To Be

Visiting my mother's house was how I met Angie and her daughter. My mom sent me to her friend Angie who lived next door because she was afraid for me and didn't want me to see what was going on at her house. Angie had a daughter around my age. My mother knew I would be happy there.

I loved visiting Angie and playing with Ameka. They became another family to me and eventually, closer to me than my own family. Even now, I call Angie when I need advice or want to talk about the old days. Back then, when I told Aunt Edwina that I wanted to go see my mom, I was lying. I wanted to go to Angie's and hang with Ameka. I wanted to watch how her mother treated her.

I wouldn't have said it then, but I think now I was a little jealous of them. Angie even told me a story about how I once stood in the hallway outside my mother's apartment, watching them like I was hungry. Little did she know, I was, but not for food.

Angie and Ameka didn't have much, but they had each other. They were mother and daughter, and they shared warmth and love and even argued sometimes. They were a family. Even though my mother's apartment was right next door, there wasn't any warmth or love there. There weren't even arguments. Think about it—you've got to care about someone if you're gonna waste your breath arguing with them. At that point, my mother didn't seem to care for anything except drugs.

I craved what Angie and Ameka had, and like a lot of young people who feel like they are missing something, seeing someone who *had* it just made me angrier. My anger made me lash out, and I took out my frustrations on the people closest to me. It made me rebellious and emotional.

So many women and girls use anger to express everything that's going on inside. They want to cry, but they don't. They're afraid that if they shed even one tear, people think they're weak and try to punk them. I know that feeling well. I know about feeling all broken up inside, but not wanting to let anyone see it for fear that if I showed I could be hurt, someone would see it as an opportunity and step up to hurt me even worse. Anger lets you mask your pain. It allows you send the message—"Don't mess with me."

I thought all the anger I had in me was something good. I thought lashing out and acting out and talking tough and asserting myself proved that I was grown. So I lashed out and acted out and talked tough and asserted myself, not with my mother or father or against the drugs or the whole circumstance, but with the people around me who were trying to help me, teach me or take care of me. Being angry brought me trouble, and it cost me the little bit of stability that I had.

From Pillar to Post

Aunt Edwina was getting too old to deal with an angry pre-teen. Her kids had all moved out and had families of their own. I don't know how it was decided, but I suspect her kids got together and discussed it. They knew their mother was getting older and that some of my most difficult years, my teen years, were ahead of me.

I moved out of Uncle Frank's and Aunt Edwina's house when I was 12. It was the only "home" I'd known since I was a baby, and now it was over. I didn't know it, but this was the beginning of being bounced from relative to relative, sleeping in shared rooms, corners and couches, for the next six years.

First, I lived with Uncle Frank and Aunt Edwina's youngest daughter, Cheryl, her husband and their two kids. Then I lived

with Frank and Edwina's son, Nat, his wife and their two kids.
Then I stayed with my Dad's friend's sister, Dionne. Then back to
Nat and his family.

I stayed with Angie and Ameka for a minute, and then it
was on to my Uncle Frank's son, Nat, and his wife, Kris. Then I
spent a few months with my mother's sister, Aunt Grace, and then
it was back to Nat and Kris. My mother's sister, Patty, took me for
a while, and then it was back to Nat and Kris.

Later, after I had my daughter, I lived with Dream's mom
for a bit, too. I even spent a month living with my mother, and
once, a whole day with my father, before his then-wife threw me
out.

I felt like a burden to everyone I stayed with. I felt like I
was in the way. Sometimes my "guardians" let me know just how
much of a burden I was.

"She's got to go", they'd say. Or they'd run me down for
eating their food or borrowing a blanket out of the closet without
permission. I felt unwelcome, not just some of the time, but most
of the time.

It wasn't until years later, when I moved to Atlanta
and bought my own house, that I finally felt like I belonged
somewhere. I knew that finally, I had a "home" because it was the
home I made for myself and my daughter.

When I was a teenager, I didn't have that safe place. It
was this person's house for a minute, then on to another one.
Underneath all of the moving around was the anger I felt towards
my parents and the hurt because neither one of them was around

for me. If they had done better, I wouldn't have been in this mess, or so I thought. If they had done better, I would have had a place where I belonged, or so I thought. If they had done better, I would have had a home.

The Mistake I Made That You Shouldn't

"They didn't want me."

That's probably what I would have said about it, when I was moving from house to house and relative to relative. I would have turned it back on them and said that those people didn't want me. But that was my younger self. The older, wiser Toya knows that at least some of the time, it was partly my own fault.

I moved from one house to the next because I was furious that I had parents, but that they weren't there for me. I moved from house to house because in most of those homes, my relatives had rules about chores, curfews, and homework, and I didn't want any part of that. I moved from house to house because I wanted to be free, just like my brothers, Walter and Josh.

My brothers were free. When I visited my mom's house, I saw how they lived. They did what they wanted, when they wanted. My mother didn't interfere with them. They were their own parents. As a pre-teen, and then later as a teenager, that freedom looked good to me compared to living with Nat and Kris and their family. Nat was like his father, my Uncle Frank. He was strict about the house rules. He wanted me to come straight home from school. He thought the age of 12 was too young for a boyfriend. He made me do my homework and he held me accountable for chores around the house.

I hated it, and sometimes, I hated him.

What I know now, and what you should know if you're young and feeling like people don't understand you and you just want to escape from all the rules and chores and drama, is that sometimes, people who really love you make you do things you don't want to do. They tell you things you don't want to hear. They make decisions that seem unfair.

I couldn't see this when I was in middle school, and you might not see it in your situation. Instead, I saw my brothers and my friends doing what they wanted. Uncle Nat seemed too strict. It felt like he was holding me back and holding me down.

I saw friends who lived with their families and had parents who wanted them. Their parents let them do whatever they wanted to. Since I didn't live with my parents, and since sometimes I felt unwanted by the people I stayed with and other times like burden to them, I felt like I shouldn't have to listen to the things those people wanted me to.

"You ain't my mama."

Like that. You know what I mean?

I don't know if I ever said that, but that's how I felt. I felt like I didn't have to listen to *anybody*. I was so angry, I *couldn't* listen to anybody.

Like the old saying goes "a hard head makes for a soft ass." My younger self didn't believe that one either, and had to learn the hard way, and I did. Searching for a home and a family in relationships with boys led me to sex before I was completely ready. I ended up pregnant at the age of 14, and things haven't been the same for me since. Being young and not having a family or a home is hard, but being young *and pregnant* without a family or a home is even harder.

Maybe your home life isn't what you wish it was. Maybe you look around you and it seems like everyone else has it good, has a perfect family, and has love and warmth and safety, while you've got nothing.

You feel alone. Maybe, like me, you feel angry.

Maybe, like me, you're throwing that anger everywhere, except at the person or people you're really angry at.

Maybe, like me, what you really need is a place to let your heart show, like I did in the pages of my journal. It was the only place I dared express just how hurt I was.

Maybe, like me, you need to know that you can't find "home" in buildings or other people. The first step to making a real home is making peace with yourself.

Toya's Priceless Gem: Home isn't a building or even other people. Home is the love in your own heart and nowhere else. It doesn't matter what drama is going on around you. Keep the faith and someday soon, you can create for yourself a home that matches the love and peace you hold in your heart.

BOYS TO MEN

Antonia "Toya" Carter

Boys To Men

Girls and young women who see my show write to me all the time, asking me to answer questions about their relationships. They've seen some of the stuff I've been through with guys and dating on the show, and they want my advice about their own situations. They ask me all kinds of questions about how to meet a guy who's about something, how to tell if a guy really cares about you, when to have sex and when to break up.

The answers to all of those questions are all pretty much the same. It's all in the people you associate with, who you hang with and what they show you about themselves. You have to learn to pay attention to what guys *say* and what they actually *do*. That's been the most important thing for me in choosing who to be with and who to stay away from. You have to choose guys who want you for more than your body, who have got something going on in their lives and who care enough about you to support the things you want to do.

How did I learn these lessons?

The same way I learned most things--the hard way. I learned from choosing the wrong guys, like the players and the pretty boys, and realizing they weren't what I needed at all.

As a person who did it all wrong, I can tell you what *not* to do and offer you these priceless gems from my experience.

His name was Mitch and he was one of the cutest boys in school.

He was in this group called The Fire Flame that danced and competed in talent shows all over the city. Lots of girls had seen him perform and lots of girls liked him. I took it up a level. As far as I was concerned, he was my boyfriend.

It was 1996 and I was 12.

I was living with my Uncle Nat, my Aunt Kris and their two kids. Uncle Nat thought 12e was way too young for a boyfriend. He was determined to keep me from getting into trouble and he was determined that I would follow the same rules that he'd set for his own children.

He picked me up every single day from school. Someone had run into the back of his car, and it hadn't been fixed yet. The back was all crumpled and he had to tie the trunk down with a piece of rope to keep it from flying open as the car moved. It was embarrassing. He would park right out front in that raggedy car and wait for me, so that everyone at my middle school could see him. I hated that; it made me feel like a baby. Every school day he did it--parked there and waited. Sometimes he waited a long time, because I didn't want to ride home with him. I wanted to walk home with Mitch, who lived near the school in a neighborhood called "The Goose." I'd slip away from the school, meet up with Mitch and we'd walk a bit, usually only as far as a little bench at the bus stop near an apartment complex called Frenchman's Wharf.

We'd sit on the bench together, hugging on each other and talking, until Uncle Nat would pull up on us and make me get into the car. I'd get in trouble every time, but nothing he did stopped me. The next day, I'd sneak out of school and Mitch and I would be at the bus stop again.

He was the first boy I ever kissed, and, of course, Uncle Nat pulled up on me and Mitch just as we were hugging up to kiss some more.

I didn't hear the car. We weren't far from a really busy street and there was all kind of noise anyway. Of course, I was all into the moment of feeling Mitch's soft lips on mine. The kissing might have gone on for a while, if it hadn't been for Uncle Nat pulling up right in front of the bus stop in his busted old car.

"Get your ass in the car," he yelled at me.

I pulled away from Mitch and scrambled into the car. I was so embarrassed. I felt like everybody on the whole street was looking at us. There was a whole group of Mitch's friends walking nearby. Mostly, I was embarrassed that Mitch had seen my uncle talk to me like that. It made me look like a little baby.

"Why you trying to be fast?" he shouted at me. "Why are you sneaking off with this little boy? Don't you know how much trouble this is gonna lead to? And you just 12 years old!" He ranted and raved the whole way home. He took away my telephone privileges and I couldn't go anywhere or do anything for a week. I had to come straight out of school and get in the car or he'd make my punishment even worse.

I took my punishment, but as soon as the week was over, I was sneaking off to be with Mitch again and finding ways around Uncle Nat's rules. I felt like I had to. All the girls had a crush on Mitch, including all the girls at my school, girls at other middle schools, and even girls at the high school where he was already a freshman. All the girls liked him. Those girls were willing to do

anything to be with him and most of them didn't have anyone
pulling them back, locking them down, or telling them "no."

Compared to them, I had so many restrictions. I wasn't
allowed to go to the movies with him. I wasn't allowed to go the
dances. I couldn't do anything. I couldn't even walk to the bus
stop!

I blamed Uncle Nat. His rules made me angry. I couldn't
wait to grow up. I couldn't wait to get out of his house. I couldn't
wait to be free to do what I wanted to do!

Since Uncle Nat didn't allow me to accept phone calls from
boys, I figured out how to get around him. Nat worked evenings
and Aunt Kris worked days. I told Mitch to call in the gap, the
hours between when Nat left for work and Kris came home.

I even figured out how to get to go out with Mitch. I lied
and told Uncle Nat I was going to my friend Sarah's house. We
were both on the dance team and I told him I would stay late at
her house after performing at the football game.

I realized that my uncle was right. Mitch was fast. I was 12
and not quite as grown as I thought I was. I was more than a little
scared by some of the things Mitch wanted to do. Mitch wanted
to have sex. He wanted to break my virginity.

He asked me to come to his house when his mother wasn't
going to be home. I thought I loved Mitch and I thought I was
ready. After all, most of the other girls at my school had already
started having sex, or at least they said they had. I was one of
the few left. Mitch knew that, too. It was one of the reasons he

wanted to be with me. He wanted to be my first.

I was gonna go, but at the last minute I chickened out. I don't know why exactly. I really didn't see anything wrong with having sex. Like I said, most of the girls were doing it. Something didn't feel right about doing it then, especially with Mitch, who had so many girls. I guess I was starting to get the vibe that he just wanted me for sex. I didn't do it.

I dated him for the whole eighth grade school year. When I got to Marian Abramson High School, the same school where Mitch went, I found out all about him and I was glad I hadn't had sex with him that night.

Mitch was a boy. Worse than that, he was a playboy, messing with lots of girls at the school, cruising around like he thought he was something. He was still trying to come around me, but once I knew I wasn't special to him, and that he just wanted *all* the girls, I wasn't entertaining him anymore.

I was disappointed in him, but I was glad I hadn't let him break my virginity. He wasn't worth it.

Toya's Priceless Gem: A boy will tell you anything to get you in the bed with him. Don't fall for it, no matter how cool he seems. If he's really cool, he'll wait for you to be ready. Don't be just another jump off. Wait for someone who loves you enough to be patient.

Keith vs. "Dream"

I know you've heard the saying "looks aren't everything."

Boys To Men

It's true. It's just that sometimes it's hard to see past a guy's looks. I used to *love* pretty boys. You know the really good-looking guys with the smooth skin, perfect hair and cool clothes. I used to love boys who had that swagger to them. I used to think the only thing that mattered was that he was pretty and I was pretty. I thought that being a couple of good-looking people would make us happy, popular and cool.

I wanted the guy that all of the other girls wanted because I thought if I had the popular boy, I would be popular, too. *Be careful what you wish for. You just might get it.* I dated pretty boys and popular boys, and dating those boys ended up being just a crazy mess for me all through school.

Keith was pretty. He was tall and handsome. He was also a year older than me and one of the most popular guys at my high school. When he played basketball on the courts near my Aunt Grace's house, which is where I was living at that moment, I'd talk with him a bit after his games. Nothing serious, but he definitely knew who I was.

We had one class together in the period just before lunch. I was only a freshman, but I used to skip out on the cafeteria and go to lunch outside the school with the seniors. One day we started talking after class, and the next thing I knew, we had left the school and gone to one of his friend's house. Almost as soon as we were alone, he started talking about sex.

I don't remember exactly what he *said*, but it was clear what he wanted to *do*. He started going on about how beautiful I was, and how much he cared about me and all that. He was kissing me and rubbing me and I was getting into it. Clothes started coming off and things got really heated.

At the last moment, and I mean the last moment, I called it off. It was happening too fast, and I guess I still didn't feel ready. I had an idea in my mind about how it should be, and fooling around at his friend's house wasn't in the plan. I didn't want to just give it up during the lunch break and go on back to school. Having sex with his friends right there in the next room made it seem like I was some kind of freak. I wanted better than that.

Keith didn't force me to have sex with him like some dudes would have done. At the same time, he wasn't happy about my saying "no." I learned later that, for him, sex was all I was about. He wasn't really that interested in me at all. I was just another girl he could brag to his crew that he'd had.

I still really liked Keith when I met this kid that everyone called "Dream." He performed in shows around town in a group. I met him for the first time right after my high school talent show. He and his group had performed, and after the show, me and some of my friends were in a nearby convenience store getting some snacks. Dream was there with his boys.

"Hey, hand me them doughnuts!"

Those were the first words he ever said to me.

I didn't know him yet. Like I said, I still liked Keith and Dream wasn't really my type. I thought he might be trying to talk to me, and I was pretty sure I didn't want to know him like that. I snatched up a pack of doughnuts and threw them at him.

"Damn," Dream smiled and shook his head at me. "If you

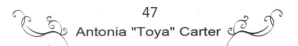

gonna come at me like that, you ought to at least get to *know* me first. Let me give you my number." He scribbled his phone number on the back of a piece of brown paper bag and handed it to me.

I found out later that he was a rapper, though he wasn't anything near as successful as he is now, and people all around New Orleans knew him. His thing was that he'd leave these raps on his voicemail and people would call him up just to listen to them. If you hit him on his pager, you'd hear his latest rap and there were new ones all the time. People would call his pager all the time just to hear the raps. He'd already been with Cash Money Records for six years when I met him in 1997.

People always think I knew about Dream's record deal when I first met him, and that I had some plan to hook up with a baller or a rapper. I really didn't know who he was or what he did. Sure, I thought it might be cool to hook up with a guy like that, but I wasn't really going out searching for that. Besides, I was 13 years old, still just a kid. Like most 13 year olds, my life was high school. I was thinking about dating the guys on the basketball team. That was my idea of a popular guy. When I met Dream, all I knew about him was that he'd just performed at my school's talent show. Even after we'd started chilling together a bit, I didn't know much about all that. I didn't ask much about it either. We talked on a different level than that. In the beginning, what I knew about Dream was just that he was charming and sweet and fun to be around. He was still not my type, but he was gentle and kind to me.

I don't remember why I called him that first time, but I did.

Then it got to be like a habit. I would hit him on the pager when he came from school. He'd call and we'd talk for hours, talking about everything you can think of.

That's how we discovered that we're related--sort of. My aunt's husband's daughter's (my cousin by marriage) uncle was Dream's stepfather. You got it? My cousin-in-law and Dream were cousins by marriage. Or something like that. We used to call each other "cousin" because his stepfather was sort of my uncle. My cousin-in-law even lived in Dream's neighborhood. I'd go over there and spend some time at her house, then I'd meet Dream and we'd spend a little time talking and kissing. He was very affectionate.

Even then, I didn't know he was as well-known as he was. At school, I had all of these girls running up in my face asking me, "Are you dating Dream?" or "Are you dating Wayne?" Depending on which question they asked, they got different answers. If they asked me if I was dating Dream, I said "yes." If they asked me if I was dating "Wayne" I said "no." I didn't know they were the same guy. It even cost me my friendship with a girl that I was tight with. She had been dating this guy named "Wayne" and she wanted to *keep* dating him 'cause he was paying her mama's bills and buying her all kinds of stuff that she was constantly bragging to her friends about. When she asked me if I was seeing him, I said "no." Then, when she saw me with him, she stopped speaking to me. She thought I was being dirty. I honestly didn't know him as Wayne. I called him Dream. To this day I call him Dream.

When I realized that Dream was the one paying that

girl's family's bills, it was the first time I realized that he had *real* money. I knew he always had cash, but I didn't know where it was coming from. He was always trying to buy me presents, things like designer backpacks to match my tennis shoes and that kind of thing. He bought me and my cousin stuff all the time, but he never said much about his money. He didn't say, "I just signed a record deal." He didn't say anything. He just kept buying me stuff.

When Keith found out that Dream was spending time with me, he only had one question for Dream--"You have sex with her?"

Dream didn't answer that question. He was a man. Keith had no business asking. He was a boy.

Toya's Priceless Gem: A real man doesn't talk about who he did what with. Only boys need to brag.

When I heard about what Keith had asked Dream about me, I was mad. I was even madder when they became friends after that. Then it went around school that I dated and had sex with guys' friends, and that I was just a jump-off who would go from boy to boy until I had dated everyone in the crew. The haters were running me down constantly, saying spiteful stuff about me. The truth was that Dream and Keith hadn't even known each other until the day Keith walked up to Dream and asked him if I'd slept with him.

All the talk and Keith and the haters actually just brought

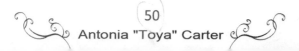

me and Dream closer together.

A little while later, he invited me on a trip to Houston with him as a part of Cash Money Record's promotion tour of his first album with *Hot Boys*. I told my Aunt Lisa a big old lie. I told her that I was staying with my cousin Demetria for the weekend, and then I boarded the plane without so much as a dime of my own in my pocket.

It was stupid and dangerous. He could have gotten bored with me and left me there, stranded. He could have gotten mad at me and dumped me somewhere with no money and no way to get home.

At the time, I wasn't worried. Dream always took care of me, and he had promised to pay for everything. He was proving himself to be everything I'd ever wanted in a man--kind and caring, charming and sweet, thoughtful and loving, ambitious and outgoing. He was young, only 15, but so was I. I believed in my heart he was the one for me. I believed that at last, I'd met a real man. I believed it so completely that I didn't care that when I got back from Houston, my aunt had called the police on me.

She found out when she caught me in a lie. I had told her that I was spending the night at my cousin Demetria's house, but then she called over there and Demetria's mom told her that we were in Houston. She didn't know I'd told my aunt that lie. Demetria's mom really thought my aunt knew where I was.

When I got home I was busted. The whole neighborhood was standing in front of my house, along with the police. Aunt Lisa had called them to get them tell me not to ever leave town without my guardian's permission again.

It was a big mess. I was angry with Aunt Lisa. I didn't feel like all that was necessary, but now I understand. If my daughter did that to me, I'd be sick with worry.

I didn't see it that way when I did it. All that mattered to me was being with Dream. We were young and we both changed as we grew older. Now, we're just good, good friends. The sweetness, the gentleness and the kindness that Dream showed me gave me a new model for what I wanted and needed from a man.

Toya's Priceless Gem: A real man can be any age. He's the one who listens to you, encourages you and doesn't pressure you.

The Mistake I Made That You Shouldn't

Because of who Dream was and how fast his career caught fire, there were lots of girls--girls who liked him, girls he liked back, girls who wanted to have sex with him, girls who he had sex with. In high school, I used to get into fights over this, sometimes really serious ones.

It was a mistake.

I can't say you should never fight. You can't let people punk you, and sometimes fighting is the only way to defend yourself. If someone puts their hands on you, then you have to defend yourself. My attitude made it worse. Instead of avoiding battles with these girls, unless someone actually put their hands on me, my attitude was the opposite. If some girl starting talking about fighting me, I'd be like, "Okay, bring it."

I entertained those girls, and of course, that was all the encouragement they needed.

Once, I got suspended from high school for a whole year after a fight with a girl who was nearly a foot taller than me and at least fifty pounds heavier.

It started over some words this girl had written about me in the restroom--"whore" and "dick sucker" and other really nasty stuff. I knew she'd done it because I heard her talking about what she'd written while I was in the stall. When I came out of the bathroom to where Dream and Keith were waiting for me in the hallway, I said something about her and what she'd written. Loud. Loud enough for the girl to hear.

"What did you say?" the girl said.

I repeated myself, with attitude. I knew where this was going to lead, but I wasn't backing down.

I said, "I don't appreciate you and your girl writing that stuff about me!" She rolled her neck at me. "And what you going to do about it?"

I hit her.

Her girl jumped in it, then my friend got in it, then my cousin joined in. It turned into a brawl right there in the hallway

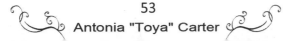

before the teachers and the security people at the school broke it up. I came out of it with a black eye, welts and scratches all over my face.

Keith and Dream just stood there. Neither one of them tried to break it up. They didn't try to stop it from happening. Why should they? They thought it was funny. They thought it was cool to see a bunch of girls get into it over them. They liked it. It made them look like they were worth fighting for, I guess, so they didn't do anything.

I got put out for a full year. I remember going home that day with my face all bloody and swollen. I was with Uncle Nat again and he just shook his head.

"Why you gonna let these girls make you ugly?" he said sadly. "Ain't no boy worth that."

Of course, he was right. I wish I could tell you that I listened to him; I didn't.

I got in lots of fights through high school, almost all over Dream. Most of them could have been avoided if I'd had a different attitude, and if I'd been less "bring it on" and more "I don't care." They would not have happened if I'd realized that any man who wanted me to fight over him wasn't really a "man" at all. Since I entertained it, and because I was ready to fight at the slightest comment or look, I ended up fighting all the time.

After a while, even Dream didn't like me fighting. He got

tired of seeing me all scratched up and bloody. I felt like I had to do it. I felt like fighting for him was one way I could prove my love.

I was wrong.

It was my mistake to think that fighting other girls would make Dream love me more. It was my mistake to think that "winning" in a fight would make me a winner in my relationship, when the two really didn't have anything to do with each other. It was my mistake to believe that I could "fix" the relationship by fighting the other girls Dream was involved with, when what would have fixed it would have been to let Dream go when it was clear he wanted to be with girls who weren't me.

Toya's Priceless Gem: When you're fighting for love, you've already lost it.

SEX AND LOVE ♡

Antonia "Toya" Carter

Sex And Love

Like most girls, I thought that if I had sex with a guy, it would mean that we were in love. I really didn't know that sex and love were two very different things. Sometimes sex and love have everything to do with each other, and sometimes they don't. Not understanding that sex and love are different, especially for guys, is one of the ways that girls get their feelings hurt.

I had sex with a guy I loved and got pregnant with his child. I watched his feelings for me change, just like I was afraid they would. I watched him cheat on me, or least have sex with other girls, even though he said he still loved me.

I got my feelings hurt again and again, because I trusted the words "I love you." Every time another girl showed up, claiming to have had sex with my man the betrayal went right through me. How could someone who said they loved me treat me this way?

My mistake was that a part of me believed it was possible for someone to both love me and treat me badly. After all, my mother and father said they loved me, and they gave me up.

Finally, after years of heartache and pain, I learned that while sex and love aren't the same, a man who really loves you doesn't hurt you again and again, unless you give him permission by taking him back again and again.

If you're caught up in a lot of drama with a guy, I can save you a lot of trouble and pain if you can follow this hard, little priceless gem:

Just stop.

Stop feeding into it. Stop chasing him. Stop fighting over him. If he loves you, he'll come back. If he doesn't come back, you've got to move on.

How do I know?

Been there, done that, and made the mistakes to prove it.

Love and Sex

I let Dream break my virginity during Mardi Gras. It hurt so much that I almost wished I hadn't done it, but by then I knew that Dream was the one I'd give myself to.

I probably could have waited. Dream wasn't pressuring me, but almost every girl I knew was already having sex. I felt like I was missing out on something. I worried that, with all the other girls being sexually active, I wouldn't be able to hold on to Dream unless I grew up a bit.

I know now that was the first mistake, doing something because everyone else was doing it and not because I wanted to do it or because I thought it was right for me. I hate to say it, but now that I'm a mother and my own daughter is getting to that age, I think it's good to wait, but if you can't wait, use protection.

I had also been lucky. A lot of girls my age had been molested when they were younger. I knew girls who had been forced to have sex by men in their families—cousins, uncles, stepfathers and even brothers. Others had been raped by their mother's boyfriends or by guys who they thought they were safe with. My own mother was raped by her sister's husband and though I didn't know it at the time, my brother Walter was *that* man's sons, not my father's. When I finally learned about that, I also understood why there was so much tension on my mother's side of my family. There were a lot secrets over there.

I had a friend who was molested by her uncle for years and years. She was in her late teens before she told and even then, she could only tell because he was dead. She was terrified of him. He'd told her all kinds of crazy stuff to keep her quiet. He said he would kill her, and that he would kill her whole family. The stress and shame of it made her a little crazy, too. I think she had post-traumatic stress disorder. You could see her just freeze up sometimes or react in ways that didn't seem normal. She needed some help, but she was scared of counseling. It was a messed up situation. She needed to try some help, but to her, getting help was as scary as the stuff she'd already been through. As far as I know, she never did get any help.

Another girl's sister's boyfriend raped her five year old niece. Hearing that story made me sick. Raping a five year old? Young mothers, you have to be careful. You can't be like, "I want to go out, and so I'll get Cousin Terrence to watch the baby." You never know. It might be the person you least expect who tries to have sex with your kids.

My closest experience to any sexual abuse happened when I was maybe nine or ten. I used to sleep on a little bed in a room that once had been the dining room of Aunt Edwina's and Uncle Frank's house, but they had turned it into a bedroom. A relative came to visit for a few weeks, and at night, he kept coming into the room, sliding into the little bed beside me, trying to touch me in places he didn't have any business. I was scared of him. I knew it wasn't right, so after the first couple of nights he tried that, I wouldn't sleep in my bed. I went to Aunt Edwina's room and begged her to let me sleep with her in her bed. Thank God she let me. I don't know what might have happened if she hadn't.

I couldn't believe that guy was trying to do that to me. He was family. He was a relative, someone I thought loved me. I didn't tell anyone, not even Aunt Edwina. Sometimes you're just afraid, and sometimes people don't believe you. Nothing really bad happened to me, but it was still enough to make me catch flashbacks. I can only imagine what could have happened. It must be terrible to have deal with being raped by someone who is supposed to care for and protect you. I can only imagine how much worse it would be to tell your mama, and have her not believe you.

I'm not an expert, but to all the girls and women out there who've been molested or who are living through being molested right now, I say find someone you can tell who will believe you and support you. If it's not your mother or your grandmother or your aunt or a teacher or a counselor, at least tell a trusted friend. You need to get the bad stuff out of your head. You need to rid of the secret and see if you can find yourself again. You've got to reach out for help. If more of us talked about these experiences, the guys wouldn't keep doing it and they wouldn't keep getting away with it because no one ever tells on them.

Sex And Love

When I had sex for the first time, it wasn't because I was forced. It was because I wanted to. I thought I was ready and I didn't see anything wrong with it. All my friends were all sharing their stories with me about the day they broke their virginity and stuff. I didn't think I'd get pregnant, but I didn't use any protection and I didn't ask Dream to use any.

That was my second mistake.

Though I wish I had waited, I don't regret having sex with Dream. He had proved himself to be sweet and thoughtful. The evening we first slept together, he called the radio station and dedicated K-Ci and Jojo's "All My Life" to me. Every time I hear the words, I think of that moment:

And all my life
I've prayed for someone like you
And I thank God that I, that I finally found you
All my life
I've prayed for someone like you
And I hope that you feel the same way too
Yes, I pray that you do love me too

After it was over, I was bleeding. Dream joked that he'd "busted my cherry" and told me he loved me. I changed the subject. I wasn't used to saying "I love you." I wasn't used to hearing it either. It wasn't something that was a regular part of my life. Dream used to get mad at me because I hesitated so much before saying "I love you" and when I finally said it, I rushed through or muttered it, rather than saying it full out.

"We been through all this and you can't tell me you love me?" he'd say.

I couldn't answer. He was right. We'd been through a lot. But he couldn't ask of me what I didn't know how to give. I didn't know yet how to give love or receive it. So I couldn't say it.

I was afraid of the word "love." I felt almost like if I said it, I'd open myself up to even more hurt than what I felt about not having a home. I just didn't like to go there.

Even after that first night, when we lay together in his bed at his mom's house, I didn't say it. I *did* do something else that was hard for me. I tried to share with him some of the feelings I'd stuffed down deep inside for so long. I told him my most personal stuff. I told him how I really felt about my mother and my father, about how angry I was at crack and the whole situation. His own stepfather had just been murdered and he sort of understood how I was feeling. Mostly I told him how I felt like my family didn't love me and he said,

Sex And Love

"You got me now. I'm your family."

The words melted my heart. They were exactly what I wanted and needed to hear. Still, I didn't tell him I loved him until months later. Looking back, I might not have been comfortable saying it, but I *know* I was in love. Not just in love, but head over heels in love.

I'd heard my friends and older cousins talking about the feeling of having butterflies in your stomach and I wasn't sure what that could possibly be like, until I felt those butterflies, flitting around in my stomach every time Dream was anywhere near me. He would come around me and my whole world would light up. He made me feel so good, and so happy. He made me feel like the queen of the whole world. I had never felt like that before. I'd never felt that good with anyone else in my whole life and I knew it was worth fighting for, worth sacrificing for.

I remember thinking. *"If this is what love is, I'm with it."* I didn't ever want to be with anyone else. I didn't ever want that feeling to end. He'd smile at me and I'd feel like I was melting inside. It was the first time I felt like I had someone who truly loved me.

I was an addict when it came to him. He was so sweet, so charming and as far as I could see, had not a single fault or flaw. I wrote my name and his all over my notebooks and on every sheet of paper inside them. I wrote it over and over, even when I was supposed to be listening to my teachers. I wrote our names and then the word "forever." I used my money to have our names airbrushed all over t-shirts, printed on my book sack, and later had them tattooed on my body, not once, but twice. I did the first tattoo when I still lived with Uncle Nat and I had to hide it from him for the longest time. When he finally saw it, he was so mad.

"Are you crazy?" he said. "Why you wanna go and do something like that? Don't you know that one day y'all gonna break up and you'll wish you didn't have that boy's name all over you like that?"

I never thought of being old or of breaking up and having to look at my ex's name tattooed on my skin. I couldn't imagine a future like that. Of course, that's exactly what *did* happen, but I was young, crazy in love and no one could tell me anything.

I know there are some young girls out there, feeling that same crazy-in-love feeling and all I can tell you is, I know *exactly* what you're dealing with. I know nothing I say, nothing anyone says, would make you believe that this love might die one day. I won't bother to try to tell you that. I do ask that you at least try to avoid one of the mistakes I made--Don't get his name tattooed on your body.

I'm telling you from first-hand experience that having a tattoo removed hurts worse than getting the tattoo. You have to keep going back, and keep going back while they burn your skin with lasers until it's gone. Trust me, it's awful and it's expensive. From where I'm standing, I would say do everything else to express your love, make t-shirts, write his name all over your notebooks, put it on the license plate of your car, whatever, but no tattoo. I got a lot of tattoos when I was in that relationship because he liked them, but most of them I wish I hadn't done. The last thing you want when you go into a corporate environment or when you have to put on a fancy dress, is to have marks all over you that make you seem like a straight up thug. I don't hate tattoos, but I just think they should be things you really, really like and believe in. If I had it do over again, I wouldn't do any of them, except maybe my daughter's name and the "I love me" that I put on my finger to remind myself to have confidence in myself when I need it.

I don't know if my younger self would have even listened to that advice. When I tell you I was crazy in love, I mean it. *Crazy.* And crazy people don't have the best judgment.

Not listening and not having good judgment were causing me other problems as well.

Dream was grieving his stepfather, but he had his mother and they were tight. My situation, though, was really messed up. I had been living with my Uncle Nat again after Aunt Lisa got mad with me for going to Houston with Dream. Uncle Nat didn't like me spending so much time with my boyfriend. Like I said, he was strict. He probably knew me and Dream were going to have sex, and he didn't approve. I didn't think anything would be wrong with it, and once we did it, I wanted to be with Dream all the time. I moved out of Uncle Nat's house again and in with another relative who lived in Bunker Hill, just to avoid living under Uncle Nat's rules. After a while, I wasn't living there either. I was staying at Dream's house almost every night as we got closer and closer.

With Dream in my life, everything was different. Dream was different. He wasn't like most of the boys I knew. The more I got to know him, the real him, not the performer he was becoming, the more I saw what a sweetheart he was. He was the kind of guy who'd do anything for the people he loved and he genuinely loved me back then.

After we had sex, I started feeling different. I couldn't believe that I had finally broken my virginity. I kept thinking about it all night next to him that first night. I remember thinking it was something special. I remember feeling more grown up.

I was also thinking about my aunties' warnings. They had been discouraging me from having sex by telling me about the consequences.

"Guys change after sex," they said. "As soon as he gets what he wants he's gonna move on to the next girl."

I was happy to be with Dream, but I was also worried and afraid about our future. Would what my aunts said be true for me, too? Would Dream lose interest in me now that he'd "had me"? Would he stop calling me, stop talking to me, and not want to see me? Would it start right away? Would it start tomorrow morning when he woke up?

To my relief, it didn't happen the next morning. He was the same sweet guy. He was also the same sweet guy the next day, and the next day and the next. Several weeks rolled by and there wasn't any difference in how he treated me. My aunties' warnings faded to the back my mind. Dream was making me believe that what they'd said wasn't true, or at least it wouldn't be for me.

In the end, though, he did change. He changed because his career took off and he was hot. He was traveling and doing things, meeting all kinds of women, more women who would do anything to say they were with him. He changed because fame changes you, and he changed because I changed.

I changed in a way that I never expected.

I missed my period, and a few weeks later, after a pregnancy test at a local clinic, I knew I was pregnant.

It was 1998, and I was 14.

The Mistake I Made That You Shouldn't

I won't make a big speech about waiting to have sex. Everyone tells girls to wait, and most of us don't. It's hard to wait when everyone else is having sex, especially if you're with a boy you like.

I wish I had waited, and I hope my daughter will. The bigger mistake I made was not using protection. After a certain

point, I knew I was going to have sex. I'd even started talking about it. I told my cousin, Akeeli, and she was really helpful.

"Let me know when you're ready and I'll take you to the clinic for birth control pills."

She did take me just like she promised, but it was after Dream and I had had sex, not before.

I didn't tell her that. She didn't know we'd already done it when I asked if she would go with me to get birth control. We went down to the clinic and the doctor did an exam before writing the prescription. They had already given me a supply of pills and we were just about ready to go when the doctor asked,

"Have we given her a pregnancy test?"

I guess the doctor knew from the exam that I probably wasn't a virgin like I'd been saying. Still, I wasn't worried. Dream and I had only had sex once. I just didn't think I could possibly be pregnant after only one time. I was wrong.

When the test came back positive, Akeeli sat down and started to cry.

"You lied to me!" she kept saying over and over. "You lied to me!"

The nurse snatched the birth control pills out of my hands. The look on her face was like "You won't be needing these, you nasty little girl."

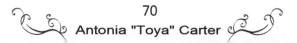

I don't think I've ever felt so low in my life.

Akeeli just kept crying. She'd been trying to help me, and I hadn't been honest with her. Now, I'd made her, and myself, look like a fool. It felt like everyone in the clinic was staring at us and judging us. It was awful.

Somehow, I persuaded Akeeli not to tell, while I figured out what to say to my family. That lasted about a day, and then she told her sister. Her sister told their mother, my aunt. My aunt told my other aunts, and one of them told my grandmother. Within days it had gone all around the family. Everyone knew, and things were really messed up.

The only good part came when I told Dream. He seemed really happy. He started talking about marriage, about being a family, and about him and me having a real life together. His mom promised to help me, too. She even seemed excited by the idea of being a grandmother. I thought, and I hoped, everything might be okay.

It wasn't.

When my aunts found out I was pregnant, they were disgusted with me. I heard them talking about me, saying that, just like my mom, I was bringing children into the world that I couldn't take care of.

"You a baby having a baby," my grandmother said, shaking her head. I felt bad because I knew she was right.

The rest of my family had more to say. They didn't want to help me raise a child. They were already mad because they'd had to raise me. Since they had to raise me, they decided they had the right to make the decision about what to do about my pregnancy *for* me. So one day, not long after they learned of my situation, they got me into a car and took me back the Family Planning Clinic, this time for an abortion.

I didn't want to have an abortion. I was scared. I knew I didn't know how to raise a baby. I knew I didn't have any idea how to be a good mother. I also knew I didn't want to have an abortion. I cried and cried. In the end, the clinic refused to do it because I was only 14. By law, the only person who could consent for me to have an abortion was my legal guardian. Since my mother had never legally given up custody of me, it didn't matter who I was living with. She was the only one who could consent for me to end the pregnancy.

At other times, the fact that my mother was still my legal guardian had been a real problem for me, especially when it came to registering for school and things like that. Only my mom could sign the papers that would allow me to start going to class, and to get her to sign them, first you had to find her, then you had to get her off drugs long enough to understand what you needed her to do.

This time, it worked out in my favor. Since she was still my legal guardian, *only she* could give consent to end my pregnancy, and it was impossible for her to give her consent anytime soon.

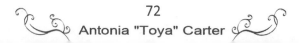

Sex And Love

She was in jail for a drug charge and wouldn't be out for another year.

I was going to get to keep my baby.

My aunts wanted me to have an abortion, so I knew I didn't have their support. Dream's career was growing and he was going to be away from me more and more, so his support was uncertain. I was still in high school and had no idea what I was going to do or how to be a mother.

I was scared, alone and terrified about everything that had to do with pregnancy and motherhood. More than once, I wished I could go back and make a different decision. I love my daughter dearly, but I for her sake and my own, I wish she had been born when I was older, more mature and had more family support to offer her. Instead, when I found out I was going to be a mother, I had nothing, not even a place to stay.

Toya's Priceless Gem: Wait for sex if you can, but when you know you're going to be sexually active, protect yourself. Don't expect the guy to do it. Always look out for yourself! After all, you're the one who will have to have the baby, and that will change your life forever!

PREGNANCY AND MOTHERHOOD ♡

Antonia "Toya" Carter

There's an old saying "the apple doesn't fall far from the tree", and it's supposed to mean that people who come from the same family are kind of alike. In my case, it isn't true.

I'm the apple that fell from the tree and rolled--and rolled and rolled. At least as far parenthood goes, I've done everything I could to be as different from my parents as night is different from day.

I'll never forget it. When the nurse put Reginae in my arms after she was born, I looked into her tiny face and I made her a promise that, whatever else I did wrong in life, I wouldn't make my mother's mistakes. I knew I'd do better by my daughter than was done by me. I'd do everything I could for her to have everything I never had and more.

From the way she's turned out, I think I've done okay so far. Reginae is about to turn 12. She's nearly at the age I was when my anger made me stop listening, when I discovered boys, and when I wanted my freedom, no matter what anyone said.

Already she says to me, "Mom you're too mean! You're too strict."

I tell her, "Mama loves you. I want what's best for you. Right now, you are still a *kid*. *Stay* a kid as long as you possibly can."

I know what I'm talking about. I was in a hurry to be grown and it didn't do me any good.

I don't know what I'll do when she starts sneaking, or when she rebels against my rules and wants to do things her way.

No matter what, though, I'll be here for her. I can't imagine ever turning her away. I can't imagine her having to go through what I went through being fourteen, pregnant, feuding with my family and all alone.

My pregnancy was really hard and I made a lot of mistakes as I tried to learn how to be a mother. I think I also did some things right. By telling you, and Reginae, my story, I hope you both can take a lesson. Do what I did right, and avoid what I did wrong.

Someone to Love Me

When I first found out I was pregnant I was scared. I wondered, *"Who's going to help me? How will I do this?"* I didn't have any idea how to be a mother, and I wasn't sure I could do it. I was still a kid. I wasn't ready for motherhood and I knew it.

Another part of me was very calm. *"It's time to grow up"*, this part of me said. *"It's time to get yourself together. You're gonna have a baby. You're going to have someone who loves you, who depends on you. You got a chance to do this right."*

I wanted to grow up. I wanted to be as mature and responsible for my daughter as I hoped I could be, but at fourteen, I still had a big mess on my hands.

I didn't want to live with my aunts. By trying to force me to have an abortion, they had sent me a clear signal about what they thought about me and my baby. While I didn't think my Uncle Nat would turn me away, I really didn't want to go to him. After all, with all his rules, he'd tried his best to prevent me from being a child having a child, and I'd rebelled against him. Now here I was, a child having a child. I was embarrassed and ashamed of myself enough without having to go back to Uncle Nat and prove to him that he'd been right after all.

I wasn't sure where else to go. My mom was in jail, so living with her was not an option. Then I thought of my dad.

He was now married and living good. He had a house not too far away, where there looked like there might be room for me. I had hoped that perhaps he'd let me stay with him and his new wife for a while. Since I'd never asked him for anything, I thought he'd say "okay." It seemed like something he should be able to do.

I went over to his house and talked to him and his wife about my situation.

"Can I stay?" I asked. I don't remember if I told him how long I would need to stay there, but I hoped that it would be enough for him to see me, his daughter, pregnant at such a young age, with so little support from my mother's side of the family. I hoped he'd think about all the years that he hadn't been there for me. I hoped that he would see it as only fair, a small payback for the years I hadn't spent with him.

He didn't answer me exactly. Instead he and his wife just looked at each other. My dad said something about "having to talk about it" and it was clear they wanted to do that in private. I got up to go take a shower. I guess I should have been concerned when they didn't say "yes" right away, but I really thought it would be okay. I thought he would persuade her. I thought he was going to explain that this was important to him. To both of us. I thought he would let her know it was something he needed to do, for both of us.

When I came out of the shower, my Dad's wife had left for work.

"She says you gotta go," my dad said.

I couldn't believe it. I just stared at him. A million angry words bubbled up out of my mouth, and I threw them in his face. I just couldn't keep them in. I think that was one of the experiences in my life that hurt me the most, realizing that even then, when I really needed him, he wasn't there for me.

Years later, he and I would talk about that day and I would find a way to forgive him. However, at that moment, I was through with him, and it would be years before we spoke again.

I went back to one of my aunts, Aunt Grace. The whole time I was there, she was talking about me, dragging me down.

"Had to be so fast, in such a hurry to grow up. Now see what you got! Knocked up by some little nigger at fourteen," she'd say, shaking her head and turning up her nose. "It's a shame. A damn shame."

Or she'd start in with, "What you gonna do when that baby gets here? You don't know nothing about raising no child. You still a child yourself!"

It was bad enough that she said this to my face, but she said this and more to anybody who'd listen. She was constantly running me down, and I knew it. Here I was pregnant, getting bigger and bigger, trying to take care of myself and my growing child, but I felt like I could never rest. Her eyes were always on me and she was always talking and talking. Everything she said was negative. Everything she said dragged me down lower than I already felt. The stress of the situation drove me out of her house. Over the next few months, I bounced from home to home yet again. From Uncle Nat and his wife, to Dream's mom, back to Aunt Grace, back to Uncle Nat, then back to Dream's mom.

All the while, I felt that Aunt Grace was right. It *was* a shame. I wasn't in school in anymore, so I was no longer doing the things the other girls my age were doing like going to the talent shows, doing the dance team and just kicking it after school. I saw Dream less than I used to because he was traveling with his new album and hadn't been home much. When he was home, I could tell he didn't like how big I was getting. He'd spend a little while with me, then hurry out to chill with girls who were still small, shapely, and not pregnant.

There were plenty of girls for him to choose from. He was starting to become really successful, and I felt like I didn't have anything much going on. It worried me. I felt the distance growing between us and remembered the warnings I'd heard.

"After you sleep with him, he gonna change." That's what my aunts and older cousins had said.

They were right.

It had taken a while, but he *had* changed.

My biggest worry was about being a mother. I hated to admit it, but my aunts were right. I *was* a child having a child, and I didn't have any clue how I was going to do it.

When I first felt the baby kick inside me, it terrified me. I knew I was pregnant, and I knew that meant the baby was in there, growing and getting stronger, but there was a part of me that didn't believe it until I felt that first kick. All of the sudden it was for real *for real.* There wasn't any getting around it. In a few months, I'd be responsible for another person.

I was big. Really big. I had a lot of complications. I had anemia and I had to get blood transfusions because of a problem with the placenta. I got real high blood pressure and had problems with fluid retention that made me swollen, sick and heavy. I kept thinking about something my grandmother said once, "Having a baby means you have one foot in the grave and one foot out."

It was true. The bigger and the sicker I got, the more I realized the limits of my body. Before, I had felt like I would live forever. I didn't believe anything could hurt me. I was used to taking chances and risks and having everything come out okay. Being pregnant made realize that, if I didn't learn to take care of myself, I might die. I realized for the first time that I wouldn't live forever.

I learned that it wasn't anybody else's responsibility to make sure that I followed what the doctors told me to do. I tried to take the medicines they gave me. I tried to eat as well as I could and to rest. It was *my* job to take care of my health for the baby's sake. I had to take care of myself.

It was hard. I was worried all the time about the baby, about being a mother, about Dream, and about what people were saying about me. The stress made me sicker, but I just couldn't stop worrying.

The months passed. I got bigger and bigger. My due date was November 28 and I had Reginae on November 29. Dream took me to the hospital. He had to leave a concert he was doing, but he came and took me. He hadn't seen me in a minute, and by then, I was swollen like Professor Klump in *The Nutty Professor* movies that Eddie Murphy made. I looked terrible.

The delivery went awful, too. While I was labor, Reginae turned around inside me. She would have been born breech, feet first, and the doctors thought that was very dangerous. I really didn't know what they meant. I just knew I was scared. I ended up having an emergency Caesarian, and that scared me too. I really didn't want them to cut me, but I understood that they had to so that Reginae could be born safely. By the time they put her in my arms, I was exhausted and weak, but I was happy, too.

She was the most beautiful thing I'd ever seen.

The day after she was born, Dream came to the hospital to see us. He took one look at me and said, "Is she gonna stay like this?"

I didn't know what I looked like, but I saw the look on his face. I guess I must have looked pretty bad.

"You're beautiful," Aunt Kris said firmly and gave Dream a disapproving look. "You just had a baby. You're beautiful."

The look on Dream's face said something different. The look on his face said I looked fat and ugly and that he wasn't attracted to me at all anymore.

That scared me, too. In the beginning, we had talked marriage. I didn't want to be a single mother. I wanted a family. I wanted a husband. Now, marriage wasn't something Dream seemed to have much interest in. He told me that he'd always be there for me, but he felt like he was too young. Of course he was. So was I. The reality is that for me, "being young" was over. I had a baby to take care of.

He gave me three rings before we actually got married. I waited because I knew he was getting the player out of him, and having his time with all these other girls. I was miserable about it.

They kept me in the hospital for two full weeks. I had to learn to walk again from the days of bed rest and waiting for the swelling in my legs and feet to go down. Finally, they let me and Reginae go home.

This time, home was at Uncle Nat's and Aunt Kris's house. Auntie Kris fixed a room for me and the baby, and friends and relatives threw me a baby shower. We did our best to settle in.

I was in love with my baby. She looked like her father, and while I had finally accepted that I was in love with him, too, my timing couldn't have been worse. He was drifting further and further away from me as he became more and more famous. I was so lonely and so sad that I poured all the love in my heart into Reginae.

She made it easy. She was a good baby and when she started talking and calling me "mama", just hearing her say my name could make my day. "Mama, mama, love you, love you," she'd say in her little baby girl voice. It always made me laugh.

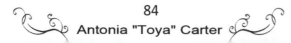

Pregnancy And Motherhood

It made me forget how hard I was struggling at school and how lonely I felt.

I took her all the places my mother didn't take me, like the zoo, Celebration Place, Chuck E. Cheese and things like that. When she was very small, she'd sleep next to me and give me kisses before she fell asleep. As she grew older, we talked about everything under the sun. I answered her little questions and explained the world to her in words she could understand. All the love in my heart belonged to her. It still does.

I was in awe of her. It was all about her. Nothing else mattered. I felt myself changing again. I wasn't worried about the things I had been worried about before her. I forgot about friends, clubs, and partying. I wanted to be a great mother. From then on, that was all I wanted to do. I didn't want her looking for a place to belong. I wanted her to always feel like she was wanted, cared for and loved. I felt like I had finally found someone to love me and I was going to do everything I could to keep her love.

Money Matters

Babies are expensive. You've got to have some money coming from somewhere if you're going to raise a child. I had no money of my own. Nothing. Dream would give me money every now and then, but it wasn't anything I could depend on. When I asked him for it, he would give it to me, and give it generously, but it was getting harder and harder for me to reach him. His career was hot, and by now he was famous. Things started to change things between us. I had to go through his mother and his friends

Antonia "Toya" Carter

just to talk to him.

It was depressing to find myself so low on his list. It was hard to remember the sweet, kind guy that I used to talk to on the phone for hours. It was hard to remember the guy who had told me, "I'm your family now."

I was 15 now and I had a child. I needed a plan for how I was going to take care of her with no high school education and no skills. I talked it over with Uncle Nat and Auntie Kris and other family, and we decided that I should go back and finish school. With my high school diploma, I'd have a better chance to get a decent job and to take care of myself and Reginae. I was also going to look for a part-time job.

I went back to high school. It wasn't easy. I was worried all the time about my daughter. Since everyone was at work or school during the days, Aunt Edwina was watching her. I couldn't think of anyone better for the job. Even though she was getting up in age, Aunt Edwina was still the closest thing to a mother I'd ever known when I was small. She taught me everything I know about diapering and feeding, then potty-training and other parts of child care. Without her, I don't know how I would have made it. I always felt like I could ask her anything, even something silly, and she wouldn't laugh or think I was dumb. When she passed away in 2005, I was devastated.

Even with Aunt Edwina watching little Reginae, I found it hard to concentrate in school. People were talking about me and Dream. Girls who were trying to get with him were always trying to fight me. I sometimes felt that I'd lost myself. Everyone was always whispering "that's Dream's baby mama" or "that's the one who says she's with Dream" and blah, blah, blah. Hardly anyone thought of me as just "Toya" anymore.

Dream made it worse. He'd sweep into town and go and be with a bunch of girls, making them think they were special to him. Then he'd come back to me, tell me he loved me and that we were gonna be together, and then leave again. Those girls would come after *me* thinking that if they could fight me and win, they'd get Dream.

It was terrible. When I finally got a car, girls would come and spray paint nasty words on it. This one girl wanted to fight me every time she saw me. Once she put it out on the public address system at a basketball game that she would be fighting me after the game. I didn't want to fight. I was looking cute that day in Gucci shirt and a fresh hairdo, but I had to fight her. She had told everyone, and I couldn't let her punk me. I lost that one and ended up going home with my face all scratched up.

Young girls think it's cool to date popular guys, rappers and ballers. You've got to know that dating those guys means you gotta deal with a lot of envious girls. I'm still dealing with that, passing comments people make out of the side of their mouths like they don't want you to hear, but they really do. Really negative, hurtful stuff. Even now that I'm making my own money and doing my own thing, people still connect me to that one relationship and have something ugly to say. Sometimes it seems like no matter how hard I try, people won't give me credit. It feels like I'm still fighting haters, and still losing.

Back in high school, whether I won or lost the fight with some girl who wanted him, Dream did what he did when he wanted to do it, with whoever he wanted to do it with. None of my fighting ever changed any of that. I know that now, but I didn't know it then. Like I said, I entertained it. I guess I thought that beating those girls would prove something to Dream, but it never did. I fought a lot in high school, and I had nothing to show for it, not even Dream.

I missed him. I missed the close relationship we had once had. I worried that Reginae didn't know her father much at all. Dream was around, but at that time, he wasn't the best father. He wasn't like what I remembered about my Uncle Frank, who worked hard at the old Woolworth's Department store, then came straight home to wrestle on the couch with his children. He wasn't like Uncle Frank who brought home pockets of our favorite candy, just because he knew we liked it and because he'd thought about us during the day. He wasn't like Uncle Frank who had been married to the same woman for decades when he died.

That's what I was hoping for, but Dream wasn't that man.

He was young, and he wasn't into it. He wasn't into the sacrifice of it all. He had to learn to be involved, and to respond to the little things that mean so much to kids. I was expecting more out of him then, but he just wasn't able to do it. *We* weren't parents; *I* was. I was the one with the baby, so I had to be more responsible.

When I talked to him, we usually ended up coming back

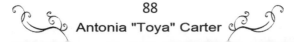

to two topics--Reginae and money. He saw his daughter when he wasn't touring and happily gave me more money than I asked for, but I did have to ask. He never complained about how much and he was never stingy about it. He still isn't that way. What bothered me was asking for it and taking it. I felt like I needed money of my own. Money I made myself.

I got a job at Papa John's, but I only lasted a few weeks. Not because I didn't want to work, but because every day it was Dream, Dream, Dream.

"He got money, you don't need to work."

"You need to make him support you and his child."

"When you gonna make him be responsible? You need to get the state on him and get your money."

The more people talked, the more I wondered if I was being stupid by slogging away at Papa John's when Dream was doing so well. While I did want to Dream to help me with Reginae, it wasn't just financial support I was looking for. I wanted *him.* I wanted him to be a father to her and a partner to me. I wanted his love. I wanted to be his only woman. I wanted us to be a family.

A check alone couldn't bring me that, and I just wasn't sure that I wanted to go to court for child support when money wasn't really the issue. The more people talked, the more I doubted myself. I loved Dream so much, and maybe I wasn't thinking straight. Maybe I *should* go to court. Maybe that would be the smartest thing to do, for Reginae's sake.

So I left Papa John's. I went to court and filed a claim for child support.

It was a mistake.

I'll never forget the hurt in Dream's voice when he called after he got the papers.

"Really, Toya? It's like *that*?" he said. "Didn't I just send you more than I promised?"

He had. I'd just gotten a generous amount of money a few days before the papers were served.

"Did you really feel like you had to do me like this?" he asked.

No. I really didn't. Dream had never given me any reason to doubt him and he'd always done what he said he would for us financially. Talking to him, I realized I'd let what *other people* said was the right thing to do guide my choices, even though I knew in my heart that it wasn't the right thing for me.

I'm not saying that our baby's fathers shouldn't be responsible for their children financially. For some people, court is the best way to make sure that happens. For me, it wasn't. The relationship we had was better than that, and Dream didn't need to be forced to pay support. I regret now that I let myself be persuaded to do something that had never felt right in my heart. I guess I was angry, too. I wanted things to be different with Dream, and I thought that maybe using child support would get his attention.

That was wrong of me. He was really doing for his daughter already, and I was letting people get into my ear. I let my unhappiness with the situation between me and Dream drive me to do something out of anger.

Pregnancy And Motherhood

Toya's Priceless Gem: Don't let people talk you into doing something you don't want to do. Only you know your situation. Only you know what's right for you.

I struggled through high school and finally finished, but I kept failing the exit exam I needed to pass in order to get my diploma. I was determined to get that piece of paper, so I kept taking the exam until I passed it. It took me two years, and I got my diploma in 2002. I was supposed to graduate in 2000. I was 19 when I finished.

The Mistake I Made That You Shouldn't

Getting pregnant messed up my chance to get my education. Although I did eventually finish high school, I wasn't as focused as I would have been if I didn't have a child at home. I was even more distracted by stupid stuff, like the things people said about me, the rumors about who was dating Dream, and my feelings of jealousy and hurt that I wasn't the only woman in his life. As I've said, I spent a lot of time entertaining the challenges of those haters when I should have been paying attention in class. If I'd been paying attention, I would have learned what I needed to know and it wouldn't have taken me two years to pass the exit exam.

If I'd paid attention, I might have done better. If I'd done better, I might have felt more confident about school and might have gone on to get a little more of it, like I hope my daughter

Antonia "Toya" Carter

will do.

Don't make my mistake. Pay attention in your classes and get your education while you can. The older you get, the harder it gets. Even if you have a baby, if you have support, go back and finish. I know it's hard to focus. Believe me, I know how hard it is, but go back and finish. Try to do your very best. You owe it to yourself and your child.

What I Did Right

Reginae and I have a good relationship. We talk about a lot of stuff, and we've been doing it since she got old enough to ask questions and listen to the answers. I don't hide anything with her. I *want* to tell her things. I don't want her to learn what I had to learn in the street. We talk about stuff like that and just girly stuff like who's cute, who's not. She likes Jaden Smith, for example. He's her Hollywood crush. We talk about how cute he is and laugh. We talk about the boy she has a crush on at school, who he likes and how she feels about it. I want her to understand that it's fine to like boys, but not to have a boyfriend, at least not yet. She knows better. She knows better because I've told her about my life. I was always sneaking around trying to do something I shouldn't be doing. Being sneaky got me in a world a trouble.

I pay attention to her schooling in a way I never paid attention to my own. When she got old enough for pre-school, I researched the choices and visited and picked the one I thought was the very best for her. I did the same when we moved to

Pregnancy And Motherhood

Georgia. I check on her homework and make sure it's done. I want her to be a good student and find out how far education can take her. My daughter has grown up to be very smart, very wise and very talented.

Now that's she older, she's really beginning to understand what I've told her about my life and how young I was when I had her. For instance, sometimes, when I go to her school, the kids ask "Is that your mom? She looks like your sister!" She laughs and I laugh, but now that she almost 12, we both know how close she is to the age I was when she was born.

If Reginae were to get pregnant as young as I did, I don't know what I would do. I try to have the best relationship with her in the world, and I hope she'd tell me if she was ready to have sex. I hope I'd be like my cousin Mary and take her to the doctor for birth control. Of course, it wouldn't be what I would choose for her.

I wouldn't want her to have a baby until she was old enough and mature enough to take care of it. I wouldn't want her to grow up as quickly as I had to.

When I think about it, it looks like I've grown up and I've turned into my Uncle Nat and my Auntie Kris who put a lot of rules on me coming up! I've come full circle, from a rebelling teen to a strict parent. I'm lucky because my daughter respects me. She knows when I'm playing with her and when I'm not. She's my daughter and my princess. I've got my family, I've got my best friend, and I've got someone to love me.

Pregnancy And Motherhood

Some people say that if you don't have someone to teach you how to be a woman, or a mother, you don't know how to do it. I don't buy it. That's just an excuse. It's how people let themselves off the hook for what they *chose* not to do. I didn't know how to be a mother, but I was determined to be a good one and I think I am. That's the point of my priceless gem about motherhood:

Toya's Priceless Gem: You can break the cycle. You. It doesn't matter what your mother did, what your father did, or what everyone else you know is doing. If you choose to do it differently, it will be different, and there's nothing more to it than that.

HEARTBREAK AND HEALING ♡

Antonia "Toya" Carter

Heartbreak And Healing

Dream broke my heart, but I have been able to move through that and build a good relationship with him. Dealing with that heartbreak taught me a lot about myself and let me move on to find a new love.

My father broke my heart, but I have been able to move on through that as well, and accept him for who he is. We've been able to talk through our feelings and find a newer and stronger relationship with each other that allows him to be a part of my life and his granddaughter's.

My mother broke my heart, but I have been able to move on through that, too. As I've learned more about the pain of her life, I've come to understand what I didn't when I was younger--that I don't have the right to judge her. Though she's still struggling to fight her demons, and I'm still struggling with my feelings, we both want to be in each other's lives. That's part of what it means to be family.

Maybe, like me, you wish your relationships were different than they are. I know I've spent a lot of years wishing for things to be different with Dream and with my parents. Of course, wishing never changed anything. In fact, wishing makes it worse, because the time you spend wishing keeps you from accepting the situation and moving on.

This, like so many other things, is something I had to learn the hard way.

Heartbreak And Healing

The Break Up

When Dream and I broke up the first time, Reginae was only two months old. I'd heard by then about all the girls he was with while I was pregnant and sick. Learning about what Dream had been doing crushed me. His feelings had changed. He would come around and barely have anything to say to me. There was a new girl who was getting his attention, so he didn't feel the need to talk to me much anymore. I was old news.

It was like he stuck a knife in my heart.

"That's it," I told myself. We broke up and it was over.

However, it wasn't over. I was still so in love with him, and we had a child together. I still needed to talk to him about her, and every time I did, all my feelings for him would come rushing back.

We got back together.

This time, I needed a place to stay yet again, so I moved in with his mom. I thought that since I was living in his mom's house, it would be easier to stay close, but wasn't. We broke up again when he started dating this other girl named Ann, and flaunting their relationship in front of me.

I couldn't believe it. I was living at his house and I had his baby, and he was dating other girls right in my face.

I felt real disrespected and jealous. Two could play that game.

Heartbreak And Healing

I met this guy named Donald who went to another high school. He had a nice car, a brand new bubble eye Lexus, and dated a lot of girls. He was interested in me. I started hanging out with him, mostly just talking and chilling. We were really more like friends than anything else. He taught me how to drive and let me vent about the situation with Dream. Donald and I were close, but there wasn't anything romantic to it. I knew he liked me, but I never let it go there. He wasn't my boyfriend, and he knew I was still in love with Dream. We used to hang out a lot and Dream didn't like it at all.

I don't know if it was the thought of me getting with Donald or if something else made him do it, but on my second Mother's Day, when Reginae was about 18 months old, Dream gave me a ring, bought me a car and proposed to me.

The wedding didn't happen. This time, Dream's career came between us. He was hot and getting hotter. He'd had his first really successful solo album and his career was turned up. Reginae and I couldn't compete with it. Within a few months the wedding was off again.

It went on like this for years.

Years.

We'd connect, then disconnect, then connect again, then disconnect, usually over some girl he was seeing. I hated those girls. I hated hearing about the ones at school and the other ones all over the country. Pretty girls, famous girls, white girls, black girls. Even though we were broken up most of the time, I felt disrespected by it. Every time I used to hear about him dating a new girl, I'd want to fight her. I started thinking crazy stuff about those girls. *"She messing up my relationship"*, I'd tell myself. *"I need to fight her. I need to show her whose man Dream is."*

It was crazy. I was crazy. The whole situation made me crazy.

It was easier to be mad at the other girls than to be mad at Dream because when Dream came home, he almost always came to see me and Reginae. He almost always wanted to get back with me and I was so in love that I always took him back. I guess I kept hoping that one day, he'd get the player out of him and settle down and we'd be happy.

No matter how mad at him I was, or what craziness was going on between us, I never kept him from seeing his daughter. I think that's a mistake some young girls and women make. They get mad at their baby's father, and then try to keep him from seeing his kid. I never did that and I don't think you should be doing it either. So many men out here never see their kids at all, and don't take any interest in them whatsoever. If you've got a man who wants to be with his kids, then that's a blessing for the child. You don't want to stand in the way of that, no matter how much craziness is going on between the two of you.

I've also seen some girls treat their kids bad because of what they are going through with the child's father, so bad that sometimes, it makes me want to cry. I mean, that's a *child*. You can't take adult business out on them. Whatever's going on between you and their father, it's not the child's fault. It's just not. I'm not preaching. I've had moments when it was hard for me to keep what was going on with Dream out of my relationship with Reginae. I've also had moments when it wasn't easy to be a good mother because I was so hurt inside that I just didn't feel like I had much left to give. I remember once, when things between me and Dream were at their lowest, I went through a period where I didn't want be bothered with nothing or nobody—not even my child. I snapped out of that real quick. I had to. I had to talk to myself and remind myself of how important it was for me to be a good mother to Reginae, and that she deserved that from me. She didn't ask to be here, and whatever stuff I was going through wasn't her fault.

Dream wasn't always the best father. He has grown into the role, but he's always tried to see Reginae and spend time with her. Spending time with her often brought us closer, because we both love her so much. That's how Dream and I got back together so many times. There was a part of *both* of us that wanted to be a family for Reginae. He proposed to me again and bought me *another* ring. I was happy and I really thought this time we'd finally be together.

Again, it was not meant to be. We broke up *again* and he went on to other girls *again*. I started another cycle of crying and hating on other girls and fighting *again*. By now, though, I was done with high school, but I didn't have much going on my life.

I spent my time worrying about who Dream was with, what he might be doing and why he wasn't with me. Other than that, I had no plans, no dreams, and nothing special I wanted to do with my life.

Was that the problem? I wondered. Was that what kept me and Dream from being together? Was it because he was living this interesting life, using his talent, doing things and meeting new people, and I was just stuck?

It worried me, but I didn't know what to do about it. I was afraid to stay where I was, but I was just as afraid to move on, knowing that Dream might come back and we might have our chance to be happy together again.

He did come back.

In 2003, when Reginae was five, he came back, claiming he'd had enough of fame and the life he'd been living. He swore he was done playing and that he wanted his family. He said those other girls meant nothing to him and that I was always the one that he'd planned to spend the rest of his life with.

He proposed to me *again*, I got another ring (the third one) and six months later on Valentine's Day, 2004 we got married in big wedding with lots of family and friends.

I wasn't expecting happily ever after, but I did hope that we would both try. I hoped that we would work together on the relationship and support each other in our goals and dreams. I

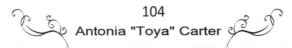

had already taught Dream that I'd be there waiting for him, no matter what he did, and he'd learned that lesson well. After only about two months, he was gone again. He wanted to move to Houston, alone, to go to college. He didn't talk with me about any of it. He just did it. No, that's not right. He talked it over with his friends, his boys, and *then* he did it. I wasn't in the picture at all.

When we talked on the phone, he sounded strange. Distant.

Soon enough, I knew why.

I started hearing all these stories about girls there and that was why he was acting strange.

It seemed like the wedding had been just a show, a publicity stunt and an excuse to throw a party. People were asking me "How's married life?" and I couldn't even answer. I hadn't even visited him in Houston.

Then, it got worse. He started getting more and public about dating other women, even though everyone knew we were married. For the first time, I felt as angry with him as I did at the other women. Things between us started to completely fall apart. I wondered what had happened to that sweet, funny guy I'd fallen in love with years before. He'd changed, and I finally realized that I had, too. I knew it was time to stop crying, to stop beating myself up about why he wasn't interested in me anymore and to stop hating the women he chose to be with.

I knew it was over. I knew I finally had to let him go.

It was one of the hardest things I've ever done. Letting go of Dream meant letting go of my girlhood dream that the three of us would be a *family*--him, me and our daughter.

As hard as it was, it was the best thing I could have done. It took packing up and leaving New Orleans and all the people there who knew me as "Dream's baby mama" or "Dream's wife", and setting off on my own to create a new life in a strange city for me to really leave it all behind me. It was worth it.

The Mistake I Made That You Shouldn't

Holding on to a dead relationship is always a big mistake. I should have let go a long, long time before I actually did.

Looking back, I know I should have moved on after the first broken engagement. Or even sooner, when Dream cheated on me the first time and didn't seem interested in really trying to make any real commitment to me. At that time, I just couldn't, or wouldn't, get over him. It made me act foolish, begging him to love me, begging him to be a family. That's what I wanted, but it's clear to me now that it wasn't what *he* wanted. The signs were everywhere. God dropped me hints all the time in the forms of those other girls, in the form of my troubled heart, in the feeling that I needed to do something for myself and by myself, but I refused to take those hints seriously until there was just nothing left.

It wasn't until after the marriage failed that I finally got over it. When I had to pick up and leave New Orleans, I started to get over him. When I had stand on my own two feet somewhere new where no one knew anything about me, I finally felt like I was over Dream. Moving to Atlanta was the best thing that ever happened to me. I finally grew up, and by growing up, I think I became a better mother and a better friend.

Toya's Priceless Gem: When a relationship is dead, it's dead and no amount of wishing will bring it back. The best thing you can do for yourself is move on, both emotionally and physically. Doing something new will help you forget the past and introduce you to some fresh experiences, and some different kinds of people.

Forgiving My Dad

After I tried to live with my father, and his then-wife put me out, I didn't have much to do with him for many years. In addition to that whole mess, I had other reasons to be angry with him.

Over the years, he had 19 kids with about ten different women. I felt like he'd been more interested in chasing women than in getting to know any of us. It was a choice I didn't respect. I'd even taken on the responsibility of raising one of my little brothers when I was seventeen and he was nine. Our mom couldn't take care of him, and my father couldn't either, so he's had a room with me in every home I've ever had. I've been the one to make sure he went to school and I've tried to encourage him in every way I could. He's eighteen now, and will make his own choices, but the point is, my father wasn't there for me or for him.

I have so many half-brothers and sisters out there that I don't even know them all. If I went back to New Orleans and started dating, I could be dating one of my own siblings and not even know it! I just feel that's wrong. I feel like my dad should have done more to get us all together at least. I feel like we should *know* each other, if we're family.

The biggest reason for my anger towards him is the impact he had on my mother's life. He was the person who introduced her to crack cocaine. If he'd never encouraged her to try it, I can't help but believe that her life, and mine, would have been completely different. Over the years, I've held a lot of anger against him for that one action, until finally I learned to accept that, "it was what it was, and it is what it is". All my anger with him and that situation ever did was hurt *me,* leaving me stuck in the past.

My dad and I finally talked it through. We did some of it on *Tiny and Toya* and talked about it some more when there weren't any cameras watching us. I just had to tell him, "this wasn't cool" and "that really hurt me."

He listened and he apologized. He didn't have a lot to say about what happened, but he understood why I was upset. For me, it was just about saying it all one time, right out loud and right

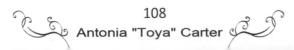

to his face, before letting the whole thing go. I needed to let go of the past and my ideas about what he should have done and what he shouldn't have done, and try to accept that he had no way of knowing that things would turn out the way they did. He had no way of knowing that what he thought would be just an experiment for my mother would turn out being a life-long addiction.

I also had to let go of my expectations for what I kind of father I thought he "should" be or what I thought he "should" be doing right now. I can't tell him he should be a different person than he is. No one has that right. It doesn't matter what I think. He makes his own choices and nothing I say will change that. I've had to accept him for who he is and hope that he'll be able to be a better grandfather than he was a father.

The Mistake I Made That You Shouldn't

I spent a lot of years thinking that I could change people into what I thought they should be or get them to act the way I wanted them to act. This is just wrong.

I'm not saying that you have to be cool with everything the other person does. You don't. You might even have to lay down some hard rules and limits on when and how the person is around you. At other times, you may have to say "no" and just walk away until the situation changes or the person makes better choices. That's not the same thing as trying to change them, judging them or being mad because they're not who you want them to be.

People aren't perfect, and trying to make them act the way you want them to act just drives a wedge between them and you. My father and I might have had a better relationship if I had been able to see him for who he was, accept what he couldn't be for me, and move on without anger.

Toya's Priceless Gem: Don't waste energy and time thinking you can change people. The only person you can change is yourself.

Forgiving My Mom

If you've seen my show, you know that my mom and I are still working hard on our relationship. My mom is still battling with her addiction, and it's important for me to support her in that effort. Addicts are very fragile and it doesn't help her any for me to beat her up for failing me when I was younger.

I'm working hard to let all of that go, just as I worked to let my father and Dream go, so we can all move forward.

Still, it's hard.

It's hard because every day that I'm with my own daughter, I wish for what might have been. I still want my mother in my life and I still want her in her granddaughter's life. I'm proud of her when she's on the right track and getting help, but I have to be strict and cut her out when she's not.

When she first got out of jail 12 years ago, all six of her

kids were in different homes, most of them unhappy, and most of them doing things they shouldn't have been doing and getting in trouble. I couldn't understand it. Why wasn't that enough for her to want to get herself together?

The answer hurt. At that time she loved drugs more than us. We weren't enough to help her stare drugs in the face and say "no." It made me sad. It made me start wishing again, wishing things could be different. As long as I had Aunt Edwina, I had someone who stood in the place of a mother for me and I was able to go on without really taking the time to find out more about my mother and her life.

Until Auntie Edwina died, I didn't know about the things that had caused my mother to use drugs. I didn't know that she was escaping the trauma of being raped. I didn't know she was avoiding her own pain. I was just embarrassed about her and, for the most part, tried not to have much dealings with her.

Every now and then, just like when I was ten and I started to visit her apartment, I'd try to connect with her. Once, when Reginae was a tiny baby and I was between places to stay, I tried to live with her.

She was in the process of getting off drugs, so I thought she wanted to be a good mom and grandmother. I hoped it would a new start for us, so we got a house and Dream helped us furnish it.

The house was designed shotgun-style--one floor with rooms going in a straight line from the front of the house to the kitchen at the back. My mother's room was near the living room, and mine was near the kitchen. Within days of us moving in, it started. There were men in the house, cooking and smoking. I was scared to death that something was going to happen to me or to Reginae. A month later, I left. It hurt me to my heart to leave because I really wanted for it all to work. I had really hoped that things had changed for my mom and me. She was older and wiser, and I had a new baby to take care of. I needed her. I wanted that mother-daughter relationship I had dreamed of for both myself and for my little girl.

Realizing that, once again, it wasn't going to happen, hurt me to my heart. However, I knew I couldn't stay. Even if I was willing to put myself in that situation, I couldn't expose my daughter to it. I just couldn't do it. I went back to stay with Dream's mom and eventually, when I finished school, got my own place.

I avoided my mom for a long time after that. When Aunt Edwina died, I really began to realize how much I needed her in my life.

It was 2005 and I had just moved to Atlanta when Aunt Edwina passed. She'd been sick for a long time and in the hospital for weeks. I had gone back to New Orleans to visit and be near her and to pray for her recovery. She'd been getting a little better, but then took a turn for the worse. Finally, we all prayed and then they disconnected the machines that had been helping her to breathe, and essentially to live. She died.

I was heartsick over her loss. She was a huge part of my

life, and I just couldn't stand it. Through all the turbulence and craziness, Aunt Edwina had always been there. She'd never judged me or called me names. She was always sweet, encouraging and gentle. She was the first to call me at midnight on my birthday. She was the one who prayed with me when times were so hard I didn't think I could make it.

She always loved me exactly like she did when I was a very little girl and she and Uncle Frank said, "We're gonna take that pretty little baby and bring her up safe, here with us."

At the funeral, I just lost it. She looked beautiful and at peace laying in the casket and it was just too much for me. I'm not one for funerals and I'd never touched a dead person before in my life, but I hugged and kissed her body. I just couldn't let her go without hugging her goodbye. She was my angel. I know she's still watching over me. I feel it. I'll see her again in heaven.

I returned to Atlanta, heartbroken and devastated. With Aunt Edwina gone, I felt like there was a hole in the foundation of my life. Dream and I were through. I'd moved to Atlanta where I didn't know a soul. Everything in my life was turned upside down. You know that song about "feeling like a motherless child"? That was me. In fact, I had never felt so "motherless" in my life.

I realized I needed to really "know" my own mother. I needed to understand her. I needed to understand what had driven her to drugs. I needed to try to find a way to bring some healing and peace to my relationship with her. I needed to stop avoiding her and accept her for who she was. I finally admitted to myself the truth that I'd been running from most of my life--I loved my mother because she was my mother. I wanted her in my life and in my daughter's life. There would always be a hole in me where she was supposed to be until I found a way to embrace her for who she was, without condoning her mistakes.

We have struggled, and continue to struggle, to build that relationship. It's been hard on us both. We've had some really great moments, and some real low points. In a strange way, I've ended up teaching her how behave like a mother. I've set limits for her, just like I do for Reginae.

She knows that I know when she's high. She knows I won't deal with that. She knows I won't let her bring random people to my house. She knows I won't let her do whatever she wants to do in my home. She's used to being down with the youngsters and partying and having a loud, good time.

I don't live like that, and when it gets out of hand, I'll put her and her friends right out of my house. It's crazy that I'm young, but I treat her like the kid. She acts like she doesn't know any better.

I'm realizing that I have to accept her for who she is, but I won't make the mistake of condoning drug use in my home. I can love my mother and hate drugs, and that's exactly what I've done and plan to continue doing.

Toya's Priceless Gem: You're nothing without your family. Building good relationships with family members, especially your mother and father, is important. Never give up control of your environment or your safety. People who love you have to respect your space and the limits you put on who's doing what around you.

DRUGS AND ALCOHOL♡

Antonia "Toya" Carter

Drugs And Alcohol

Most of us try drugs and alcohol because we're with people who are doing it. They make drinking and getting high look cool, fun, and the thing to do. That's the only reason I've ever tried any drug at all, simply because everyone else was doing it. It was a dumb reason and the experience was a disaster. I'll never do anything that stupid again, regardless of who else is doing it. It's just not worth it.

I was reluctant about trying any kind of drug. I knew I'd never get anywhere near cocaine or crack, especially knowing how quickly my mother had gotten hooked on it. I know some people would have said, "Well, that's *her.* That's not going to happen to *me.*" However, I was scared. My mother probably thought the same thing herself when she tried it. I'm sure she never would have touched that pipe if she had any idea what it would mean for her future. I'm sure my father never would have brought that stuff in the house if he'd known.

That's just it--you don't know. You don't know if you'll be able to use it sometimes and be fine. You don't know if you'll use it once and love it so much you become an addict. You don't know if that stuff you're sipping, or popping or smoking or needling will kill you. You just don't know.

Fear of ending up like Mom kept me from taking chances with any drug or with alcohol, but I did experiment. Once.

Me and XTC

Everybody was doing it.

I mean *everybody*.

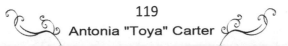

There were a few years there where it seemed like everywhere you went, people were popping Ecstasy (or XTC or X).

I guess X is still pretty popular, but there are so many other things people mess themselves up with, like pills, steroids, and marijuana. When you go out, it's like those and other things are the things to do.

I was still in high school and me and some of my friends had gone to a Halloween party at someone's house. We were all just hanging out and chilling. Everyone was popping X, talking about how good, peaceful and happy it made them feel. I figured "why not?" I wanted to feel good, peaceful and happy, too. I wanted to be able say that I'd done XTC and it was great. I didn't want to be the only baby in the room, too scared to try it when everyone else was getting high. It looked to me like everyone else who tried it was having fun. I wanted to have fun, too.

I already knew my tolerance for drugs and alcohol was really low. When I tried pain pills for a tooth ache I would feel really high and when I tried to drink, it seemed like only one would really affect me. Two drinks and I felt like I needed to go to sleep. Knowing that I could barely handle alcohol, I should have known better than to even try anything harder, but I didn't.

I tried it anyway and about an hour later, I was hallucinating. I know most people feel relaxed and extremely happy and good on ecstasy, but it got me in the opposite way. I started freaking out. I was sure someone was after me, wanting to hurt me or rape me. I got so upset and out of control, my friends had to leave the party to take me home.

Drugs And Alcohol

As bad luck would have it, we got stopped by the cops on the way to the house. I was laying with my head on someone's lap, I don't remember whose it was anymore, and they were doing their best to keep me from screaming, shaking and acting like I was crazy. If I'd jumped up and done that while the police were talking to the driver, the officers would have known that I was high and the whole group would have been in trouble.

I didn't jump up and my friends didn't get in any trouble. We made it to the house without anything else happening, and by then I felt a little calmer. I was done hallucinating and now I wanted to talk.

I talked and talked. I told *all* my business, and things I would normally never tell came spilling out of me. I had gotten a name tattooed on my thigh and I was telling all the details of why I did it, who did it, when and how much. I kept talking and talking until everyone was tired of listening to me.

Then I couldn't sleep. I was up all night and all the next day. Finally, I was so tired I was just lying on the floor, staring at the ceiling. I couldn't focus enough to do anything.

It was a horrible experience. I know I'll never do anything like that again. Never. Ever. Ever.

Fortunately, I was with people I knew when it happened and they tried to help me. I would never even think of trying something like that, something that takes you out of your mind, with people I don't know well. Drugs and alcohol make you very vulnerable, and you wouldn't want to be experimenting with something like that in a place that's unfamiliar or without good friends around who care about you in case something goes really, really wrong. Lots of girls have gotten into bad situations when they got too drunk or too high around men they didn't know well.

Don't let that happen to you.

I know so many people who have to get high just to have fun. For real? If that's true, it's the saddest thing I ever heard. Or I've heard girls say they do it to please their man. Girl, please. You shouldn't have to do things like that to please a man. I'm sure that was part of the reason my mom got hooked. She did it because my father asked her to. For some people, popping a pill or drinking that "lean" is like chewing gum. I had a friend whose lean habit helped her get diabetes.

Not good.

The Mistake I Made That You Shouldn't

I guess at some point, everyone's gonna try this stuff and find out what it's all about. I was no different, but I wish I'd been of a stronger mind about resisting doing something that I knew wasn't for me.

Now, I'm a glass-of-wine type girl. I don't mess with hard liquor, or anything mixed. I remember I had a shot of Patron on one of my birthdays. Never again. I'll just stick to my Riesling, or my Muscato. That'll do the job for me just fine.

While I do hang around with people who smoke, marijuana is not my thing. I'm not offended by it either. To me, it's like people around me who drink hard alcohol. It's fine for them; it's just not for me.

Drugs And Alcohol

Harder drugs? I don't want them around me. I hate drugs, I hate drugs, and I hate drugs. I can't be more plain that. I don't use them and I don't want to be around people who do.

What I Did Right

I don't drink in front of Reginae, and I won't let anyone else smoke or drink in her presence.

I can't believe how many people abuse alcohol and drugs right in front of their children. It's like they don't understand that the kids are watching and thinking "that must be cool, because Mama/Daddy is doing it." It's like they don't know, or care, that they're setting a terrible example for their kids.

Once, I was getting my hair done at this little salon and one of the girls working there was smoking weed in front her kids. The five year old kid was imitating the adults! I knew I had to get out of there before I said something that might have ended in a fight. They were teaching the kid that it's cool to smoke and I think that's wrong. Just wrong.

I don't know for sure, but I don't believe that everything is genetic. I don't believe that just because your dad was abusive or your mom drank means you have to end up the same. It's a choice, and to say anything else is an excuse. My parents were addicted, but I'm not strung out. You have to choose not to go down that path, and if you do choose it, then that's *you,* not your mama or your daddy or anybody else. It's all in the person. You don't have to be anything your parents were.

You get to decide whether you're gonna play with that stuff or not. I hope you decide to leave it alone because for a lot of people, no good comes out of it.

Toya's Priceless Gem: Have a strong mind about drugs and alcohol. Don't let anyone pressure you, especially if you have kids. It could ruin your whole life.

DOMESTIC VIOLENCE♡

Antonia "Toya" Carter

Domestic Violence

Verbal and physical abuse haven't been a part of any of my relationships, but I've been touched by the damage they can do.

A good friend of mine was killed by her ex-boyfriend. Shawnte was shot as she returned home from a date with another guy. I guess he figured that if he couldn't have her, no one would. The saddest part came when we realized that he'd been abusing and terrifying her for months, and she didn't tell any of us.

It's hard for me to talk about this. It's painful to think about what she'd gone through and how a twisted man's idea of "love" wasted her beautiful life. I'm probably gonna either cry or throw up while I talk about this one, because it makes me just that sick and just that sad.

I'm gonna tell it anyway, because it's important. Too many girls and women think that abuse is a part of love. It's not. It never has been and it never will be. If you're with a man you're scared of, you need to find someone to tell, someone to trust, and some way to get far, far, away.

Shawnte would want me to tell her story, in hopes that it might help someone.

Please listen and don't let her story become yours.

Shawnte and I had known each other for years, but for the first few years, we didn't like each other. Now, I would call it silly stuff. It was some drama over some guy I had dated for a minute that she started seeing and we went back and forth over him. Back then, that boy-drama was enough to keep us from having much to do with each other.

Just before I left New Orleans for Atlanta, and a little before Hurricane Katrina hit, we started seeing each other more. She was living at the same apartment complex I was, and we ended up hanging out more and more. We'd see other at school games, call each other "cousins," and things like that. By then we'd both grown up a bit and we were over the silly, jealous girl stuff. She was doing good in her life. She'd bought a condo and car and she had a good job. I had Reginae and was married and was doing my best to get myself straight, too.

When I moved to Atlanta, Shawnte promised to come see me. I hoped she would. She had become one of the friends who I really enjoyed spending time with. By the time I left New Orleans, there were only a few of them left. You remember I wrote about it earlier. New Orleans had become nothing but drama for me and there weren't too many people I thought I would miss by leaving. Shawnte was one of them.

I left and got myself settled in Atlanta. I hadn't talked to Shawnte in a while because I was busy trying to get my life together once I knew Dream and I weren't going to make it.

Then Katrina hit and for all of us who are from New Orleans, nothing was ever quite the same. I heard from Shawnte a few months after the storm and she wasn't doing so good. Katrina had destroyed her car, and though her condo was still standing, she felt like it was time to leave the city. She told me she'd already found a tenant for it and that she'd like to come start fresh in Atlanta.

Domestic Violence

"Can I stay with you for a minute?" she asked.

I didn't hesitate.

She moved to Atlanta, stayed with me for a while, and I helped her to get herself together in a new town. I was pretty familiar with the city by then, and I remembered how it had felt to get there and not really know anyone, so I was glad to help. Mostly, I was happy to have a friend from home with me in Atlanta. We hung out and had fun. We double-dated---a guy named Zach for me, his friend Al for her. It was good, but just fun. Nothing serious.

Then Shawnte and I had a falling out.

She was hooked on some guy back in New Orleans (I don't know how they met) who told her he was separated, but he wasn't. I knew he was married and living with his wife (a cousin told me), but I didn't know how to tell Shawnte that. She was so happy with this guy. He gave her a ring and sold her a bunch dreams about marriage, family and home. Meanwhile, another friend back in New Orleans was telling me about how this same guy was going around telling everyone how he had Shawnte hooked on him, how she thought he was getting divorced, but he wasn't, how he found some ring in some wreckage after the storm and gave it to her, and how she was stupid enough to think he bought it and that it meant something.

I was torn. My friend in New Orleans was telling me one thing, and Shawnte was with me in Atlanta saying something else.

I didn't want to tell her the bad news that her "relationship" was a sham and I didn't want to put my friend on the spot for having told me. It seemed smartest not to say anything, but I hated seeing Shawnte fall deeper and deeper in love with a man who didn't care anything about her.

I didn't know what to do.

I ended up turning to one of our mutual friends for advice. That was a mistake. Instead of advising me, that woman told Shawnte that she was being played, and worse, that I knew all about it and had just let it go on! Shawnte was furious with me.

"Why didn't you tell me? Why would you go and tell someone else my business like that and not tell me?"

She was so angry, and I felt really bad. I hadn't meant for her to find out like that and I couldn't believe the woman I had turned to for advice had stirred up this entire mess.

Shawnte was distant for a while after that, and when things thawed out again, she had changed.

Strange Men

She met the guy that killed her at a local park during an event called "Glenwood Day."

We weren't as close as we had been, but I was glad she wasn't mad at me anymore. She kept talking about her new boyfriend but some of the things she said sounded weird to me.

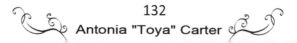

Domestic Violence

She said he kept comparing her to his mom, saying stuff like, "You're like my mom. I don't know what I'd do if I hadn't met you. I don't know what I'd do without you."

It just didn't seem like something most guys would say, but the guy's mom had just passed, so I thought maybe he was just missing her.

When I met him, though, I thought he seemed strange. I'd usually liked her guys. I didn't feel much more than that about him, though. It wasn't anything dramatic. He just seemed a little odd. However, they were happy, so I was happy. It was okay. He moved in with her and for a while, it seemed like they were good. They seemed to be doing well.

Before too long, though, he started doing little crazy stuff. He didn't want her to go out without him. He wanted her only around him. He didn't want her to have any friends. He'd be tripping when she did come out to hang with us. Shawnte didn't like how possessive he was and she was getting tired of it. Worse, he'd lost his job. She ended up working two jobs while going to school, while he sat at home, counting how many minutes late she was running and jumping all over her as soon as she walked in the door.

She started feeling like, *"If I'm doing all this by myself, then I should just be by myself. Why am I taking care of this man?"*

She stopped telling her friends about what was going on

with him. Later, I heard some terrible stories. For instance, I heard that once he locked her in a trunk to keep her from leaving. I also heard that he put his hands on her when she tried to break up. She was bartending part-time at night at a strip club, and working by day at Loomis Fargo, the armored car and security company. Loomis Fargo was a great job, with a good salary and benefits and she had been really happy there. She suddenly quit. No one could understand it because she really loved her job and had been proud that she got it. We learned the reason after she was dead:

Her man wanted to hit a lick on one of the trucks and use her inside knowledge to keep from getting caught. Shawnte wasn't going to let him rob an armored truck, so she quit before he could finalize any plans and she ended up working full-time bartending at the club.

A month before he killed her, she called the police because she wanted to put him out. The police wouldn't put him out because he was on the lease, and they suggested that maybe she should leave until things calmed down.

She came to my house and wanted to sleep there. I knew something wasn't right, something more than just her wanting the police to evict the guy, but she wouldn't say anything more than that. She wouldn't say how bad it really was. All she said was, "I want him out."

A few days later, it looked like they had worked it out.

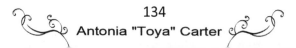

Domestic Violence

They took a trip to Mexico for a long weekend and when they came back it seemed like they'd reached an understanding. I guess she must have told him he could stay, but they were just roommates. I don't really know what happened. All I know for sure is that she started dating again.

Her ex-boyfriend/roommate stalked her.

She didn't know he was watching, but he was.

Last Night, Last Words

I talked to her on the night he shot her.

She was going on a date with one of the guys she met while bartending at the strip club and she called to say she was going to miss a karaoke night with us girls.

"Be safe," I said.

"I will," she said.

"Love you, friend," I said.

"Love you, too," she said.

We hung up. The next time I heard anything about her, she was in the hospital, fighting for her life.

She went on her date, not knowing that the whole time, her ex was following them, watching. After she said good night to her date, her ex walked up on her and shot her right in the head.

Then went to his mother's grave and shot himself.

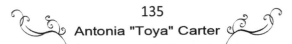

Domestic Violence

I got a call from the police. I'll never forget it. I was driving a friend to the airport and I nearly lost control of the car. I couldn't believe it. I couldn't understand it. I was like "Why? Why her?"

As the details started coming out, I finally understood just what she'd been going through over the last few months. She'd told little bits to different people, a bit to her mom, a bit to this friend and that, but it wasn't until we all got together, sitting in the waiting area at the hospital, praying and praying that she would make it that we started to get the full picture. The guy had been violent, abusive and crazy. He was so crazy in love with her that he'd decided to kill her if he couldn't have her.

You don't want anyone to love you like that.

I couldn't see her in the hospital. She lived for two weeks, fighting the whole way, but I couldn't bear to go in and see her. It had been explained to me how she looked, how the bullet had torn up her face and how the surgery had swelled her head, and I just couldn't do it. I wanted her to remember her the way she was--a beautiful girl with a body to die for, the tiniest waist and big pretty hips and the brightest, happiest smile.

I couldn't stand to see her all swollen and torn up, but I went to the hospital every day, praying and waiting and the whole nine.

She didn't make it.

She died at the age of 24.

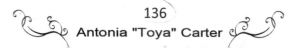

Antonia "Toya" Carter

I cried and cried.

It was a crazy, crazy, situation and the whole thing just broke my heart.

Years later, I met a girl who worked at the doctor's office, and she reminded me of Shawnte. It wasn't just her face, but it was something else I couldn't put my finger on. When I got a call a few months later from the doctor's office, telling me about this girl's funeral arrangements and learned that she, too, had been killed by her boyfriend when she tried to leave, I understood. She was sending off that same vibe, that same energy. She was another victim of domestic abuse.

Shawnte's Mistake

I feel bad saying that my friend did anything wrong. She was a victim who didn't deserve what happened to her. If there was anything I wish she had done, and that I hope would have saved her, it would be that I wish my friend had spoken out. I don't know if we could have saved her, but we could have tried. We would have gotten her to one of the women's shelters that specialize in abuse. There are listings for them in your phone book and online if you need help. We would have called the police and other people who are experts in how to handle men like this. We would have used our resources to help her get away, as far away as she had to go to be safe.

Did you know that women are more likely to be killed by a

Domestic Violence

boyfriend, husband or ex than by a stranger? When he says he'll kill you if you leave, look out. Get help. Tell someone. Don't be afraid to go to a shelter or the police. The statistics say that if he says he will, he really just might.

Don't laugh it off. Take it seriously. For real, it could happen to you.

Don't laugh off verbal abuse either.

I've seen so many women just shrug it off when their men call them out of their names. My cousin's baby's father can't call her anything but "bitch" or "ho". He tells her to "shut the fuck up" right in front of the kids.

I'd never let a man talk to me like that. In front of my kids? No, baby. That's *not* love. It's disrespectful and it's teaching the children that it's okay to talk to their mom that way. I don't know why she tolerates it, but she does. She just laughs. I guess she thinks it's okay. I guess she thinks it's just talk.

I've noticed that some women seek out that type of relationship. They simply love abuse. Don't be one of them.

As for me, I hate that kind of relationship and I won't be a party to it. In some of the homes I lived in as a kid, the man and the woman would go at each other like it was a boxing match.

I'd call the police every time. They'd be fighting, and I'd be hanging out the window yelling "Help!" When they start swinging

Domestic Violence

licks, I'm out. Sometimes, they'd get mad because I'd be calling the police, or yelling my head off for someone to come. "Don't be putting our business in the street like that," they'd say.

"Then don't fight in front of me," I'd say. And I still say that. You fight in front of me, I'll put everyone in the house on blast. I'll tell all your business. I won't stand for a man hitting on a woman or a woman hitting on man, especially in front of children. I just won't.

If a man even looks like he's *thinking* of raising a hand to me, it's over. If he ever touched me, I'd call the police, yell for everybody in the neighborhood and call everybody in my family. I would never keep a secret like that, and I don't care what you threaten me with. I'd never forgive him either. A man who hits you once will do it again.

You hear me?

If he hits you once he will do it again. It doesn't matter how sorry he is, or what he promises. Don't fall for it. Don't get caught up in the cycle. Don't end up like my friend.

Please.

Domestic Violence

Toya's Priceless Gem: Physical and verbal abuse are NOT love. If your boyfriend or husband or baby's father is abusive to you, it's time to get out of the relationship. Call the police, call a shelter, tell a supportive friend or family member. Be smart and safe, and get help before you get away, but do get away. Your life might depend on it.

MONEY AND FAME ♡

Antonia "Toya" Carter

Money And Fame

We all need money, but I believe what the Bible says-- the love of money really *is* the root of all evil. Everybody needs money to live, but I'm not the type of person who is money hungry.

I know some people don't believe that. They think that because I was married to Dream and we have a daughter together, I must have been gold digging from the beginning. It's not true. When I first met Dream, I didn't even know he was in music seriously, and I certainly had no way of knowing he would have the career that he ended up having. I just thought he was funny and sweet. It didn't go any deeper than that in the beginning.

Even after he became more successful, it wasn't about the money. I wanted to marry Dream because I loved him, not to get my hands on more of his money. There was no reason for me to be like that because he'd always been generous to me and to his daughter. For me, it was always about love, pure and simple.

Some people I've known, and even members of my own family, don't see it like that. Some people are money *hungry*, and if they find someone who has some, they'll latch on like blood suckers. If they were in my situation, they would have had every penny Dream ever made, and be mad at him because there wasn't any more.

Although I've never been money hungry, I haven't always been as independent as I am now. It took me a long time to figure out what *I* wanted to do, what I was good at, and what I liked.

Money And Fame

While it's nice to spend other people's money, spending *my own*, without having to ask anybody for it, or explain how I plan to spend it, is the best feeling in the world.

I've never sought fame either, but I've learned some things from it, too.It's nice because I get some pretty amazing opportunities to go places, meet people and do things, but it has its down side, too. For a long time, I wasn't known for anything other than being Dream's "baby mama." I hated that. I hated not being known for myself, but instead only for who I used to be married to. This made me feel like I wasn't worth anything on my own. It made me doubt myself.

Like money, fame attracts both users and scary people. It sometimes brings out the worst in the people closest to you, too. Sometimes it brings out the worst in people you'd never expect to act that way. If money and fame are what you're seeking for yourself or through a relationship, you need to be careful. Things aren't always what they seem.

Ballers and Rappers

I know for a lot of girls, it's all about getting a guy with money. They want to be with a baller or a rapper for the fancy things he can give them and the lifestyle he can provide. I can tell you from experience how people treat you when they know they're in charge. When men feel like they have power over you, they treat you like crap.

Money And Fame

For years and years, I had to go to Dream for everything I wanted. As I've said, he was good about it for the most part, but every now and then, he'd be upset with me about something and I knew I couldn't ask for anything. I always had to think, "Is this a good time for me to ask?" I had to be always thinking, always figuring out how to put it, and always guessing what his mood was so I could be prepared to deal with it. If he thought I'd done something, or if he was mad at me for whatever reason, I wouldn't get what I needed. I always had to wait on him to decide what he wanted to do.

It was *his* money, not mine.

Don't get me wrong. It's nice to have a guy who has money, and it's nice to have a guy who wants to do for you. Like I said, I'm not money hungry, but I don't want a broke guy either. I want someone who is ambitious, and who is doing things and making money, like me. I want someone who can do things with me now, but who's also thinking about the future enough to be planning to grow old with me.

As good as it is to have a man who can provide, it's just as important to be able to do for *yourself*. Then you'll never be in the position that a lot of baller girlfriends and wives find themselves in, where you're begging all the time, or even worse, where he gets tired of you and then you're cut off and you've got nothing to fall back on.

Since I started making my own money, I don't have think

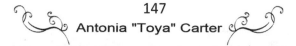

about anybody's mood but my own. I don't have to ask. I spend what I need to spend when I need to spend it. I can't tell you how good it feels.

I can't hate or knock girls who are looking for a baller or a rapper, but I wouldn't encourage *anybody* to depend on a man. It's best to have your own, too.

Some girls go really far in their efforts to get a guy's attention, thinking that if they dress a certain way or do certain things sexually, it's going to keep a man. What they don't understand is that ballers, rappers and guys like that get women to do all kinds of stuff to them and for them all the time. It doesn't mean a thing to them other than a good locker room story. It won't make them make a commitment to you, and they'll have another girl doing the same thing to them tomorrow.

Don't embarrass yourself by being slutty, or acting like some kind of freak. If you do get a baller or a rapper that way, you can be sure you'll only have him for that one night. There's no way he's going to wife you up.

Instead, it makes more sense to be yourself and to show some self-respect. If he likes you for being you, then maybe you have a chance at something more.

On Fame: Can You Listen To My Mix Tape?

Fame has definitely been a mixed blessing for me. I can't escape from that one relationship that first put me in the

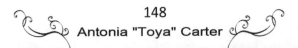

spotlight. I can't help who I fell in love with, but that's over now and it's not the only thing I have going on. My new show, *Toya's Family Affair*, is just about me. It's not about Dream at all. My boutique "The Garb" is something I'm doing on my own. I didn't name it "Dream's Baby Mama's Place" trying to build off of him and his name. Even with this book, I didn't write some tell-all, Dream-bashing story. I wrote about me. Dream is a part of the story, but only a part.

Sometimes I feel like I can't get any credit for any of the things I've done on my own. I can't get credit for choosing not to live my life completely in the shadow of my relationship with Dream. I'm famous because of who I fell in love with, even though it's something that I couldn't help.

Being well-known is cool. It's brought me some pretty wonderful opportunities. It almost feels wrong to complain about any part of it. There are definitely times when it gets tricky. I try to let those moments just roll off my back, but every now and then, something really upsets me, or really scares me.

Everywhere I go, nearly every day, I meet someone who thinks that, because of who I'm associated with, I can help them with their career in music. Sometimes it's people on the street, or it's a friend of a friend, or even I guy I might have gone on a date with.

"Toya! Can you listen to my CD?"

"Toya, can you get that producer you know to sign me?"

"Can you get Dream to listen to this?"

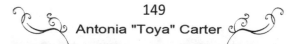

Money And Fame

"Bring Dream to my show!"

I have to keep explaining that I have nothing to do with that. *I'm* not in the music business. Dream is, but I'm not. I can't just hand him the stuff people try to give me. That would be like me telling him how to do what he does, and I'm not going to do that. It's not my place and it's disrespectful of everything he's had to do to get where he is.

When I try to tell people this, they get mad at me sometimes. They feel like I should try to help them get started in the business, and when I won't do it, I'm being stuck-up or full of myself.

Here's the thing they don't get. From what I've observed over the years, hardly anyone really gets a career because they know someone or they are related to someone. Getting a career in music requires the same things from everybody. You've gotta get out there and hustle. You've got to build a following. You've got to show that enough people like what you're doing and that you will make the label money. You can have mad skills, but unless you've got a fan base, it won't matter much.

Like most things in life, you can't expect someone else to do it for you.

I had to say this to my own brother. He's a rapper and he's definitely got skills. He came to me and he was like, "Toya, you gotta give my stuff to Dream and put me *on*. You gotta give my stuff to your producer friend."

I had to tell him that I couldn't do it and I had to tell him

Money And Fame

why. He was pissed with me, but I've just made that a rule. No exceptions, not even for family.

I know my brother will make his way because he's good, because he's grinding, and because people like what he does. Just like with money, it's better when you know *you* have earned it.

So please, if you see me on the street one day, don't ask me to hook you up with Dream or with the producer I know. Just say "Hi Toya!" and leave it at that.

Stalkers and Crazies

People see me on TV and they feel like they know me. This is good in a way. I'm glad my show has touched so many people, and in a way, they *do* know me. I'm 100% myself on the show. What you see is my life, for real.

However, you don't see everything, and the things you see on camera are only a small part of what goes on and of who I am. Although I'm grateful to the millions of people who have tuned in to watch *Tiny and Toya* and to watch the new show, *Toya's Family Affair,* I don't know them as well as they know me.

Most people understand this, but sometimes I meet people who don't.

"Hey Toya!" they'll say, then start talking to me like I'm their best friend. Then they get mad when I don't respond that way. I can't help it and I really am sorry. I don't mean to be conceited or rude. I just don't know them.

Then there are the guys who watch the show and decide that they are the ones for me. These guys are much scarier, because sometimes they follow me around or try to touch me.

Once I met a guy like this who made me so nervous I thought I was going to have to call the police.

"Toya, I love you. I wanna take care of you. I'm gonna treat you right."

He just went on and on, and he wouldn't quit. I finally got away from him and got in my car to go home, but when I looked in the rear view mirror, there was someone following me.

My little brother was in the car with me that night.

"Pull into that gas station," he said.

The car pulled in right behind us and my brother jumped out. It was the same guy who had just professed his love for me, now following us in his car.

My little brother took serious action.

"Leave her alone!" He was screaming at the top of his lungs, and people were looking at him like he was crazy. He probably did sound crazy, but he was trying to help me. He was trying to scare the guy into leaving. "Get away from her or I'll call the cops!" he shouted, pounding on the guy's car.

That did it, and my stalker zoomed off. I didn't see him or that car any more on the rest of the drive home, but I was still all shook up by that. I live by myself and I only have security guys around me when I travel and do events. That was the incident that led me to first start thinking that maybe I needed to own a gun, and learn how to shoot it, just in case I found myself in a situation where I needed to defend myself.

I did get a gun, and I've taken some classes on how to use

it. I've been to the shooting range a few times, but I'm not sure that was such a good idea. I want to be safe and I sometimes feel like I need more protection, but I'm just not comfortable holding a gun. I've realized that too many people I've known have gotten shot and this has made me terrified of guns. I haven't decided what I'm going to do to feel safer from stalkers, but I'm going to have to do something. You can't be too careful.

Toya's Priceless Gem: Dating ballers and rappers is fine, but remember their fame and their money are theirs. It's so much better to have your own. No one can ever take that from you.

FRIENDS AND USERS ♡

Antonia "Toya" Carter

Friends And Users

Everybody's got some fake friends, and it doesn't matter where you are in life, there are always gonna be people who only like you because of what you can do for them, what you've got, or who you associate with. Even before I had a television show, and even before Dream was as big as he is today, there were girls who only wanted to be friendly with me because they thought they could get something out of it.

You know what I'm talking about. Some girls want to hang with you because you're pretty and they think you can help them get guys. Some want to hang with you because you're smart and they want you to do their school work, or because you've got cute clothes and they want to borrow them. Still others want to hang with you because you have some money to spend and they don't have any.

Now that Dream is so well-known, a lot of girls want to be my friend because of him, even though we aren't married anymore and I don't see him that often. They're really nice at first, but before too long, they start asking things like "When you gonna see Dream?" and "What's he like?" and "Can I meet him?"

It's happened to me so much that I'm a whole lot more suspicious of people than I used to be. It's harder for me to trust than it used to be, and I take longer to get to know people before I call them "friend." I've learned to be real careful about what I say out in public, even if it's just chatting with the girl who's doing my hair. There are some sad and crazy people out there, and it seems like every single one of them has a blog. I don't want anything that I say to come out on the Internet all twisted into something I don't recognize. I know it sounds paranoid, but if you've ever had someone start spreading some lies about you on the Internet, you know how I feel.

So when I first meet someone new, and even when I talk to my old friends, or friends I've had since middle school, I'm careful about what I say and how much of my business I share. I don't know if this is a good thing or a bad thing.

What I do know is that friendship, true friendship, is very, very important to me. In trying to find and keep true friends, I've made my share of mistakes. Here are some things I've learned that I hope can help you sort out the fake from the real in your own friendships.

Hanging With the Older Kids

Growing up, I didn't have many friends, and most of the friends I had were older than me, sometimes by only a year or two, and sometimes by four or five years. When you're a kid, even a year or two of maturity makes a big difference. There's a big difference in what you might be doing and feeling at ten than at 12. There's a big difference between twelve and fourteen, and a big difference between 14 and 16.

When you're older, age doesn't matter as much and it's easy for a 25 year old and a 30 year old to be close. However, being 13 and hanging out with girls who are 17 or 18, makes for a big difference in what's legal, acceptable and appropriate.

I would have argued with you about this when I was 12 or 13. I would have said that I was plenty mature and I was cool

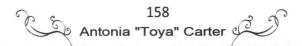

with hanging with people older than me. Now that my daughter is about this age, I can say with absolute certainty that I wasn't ready to hang with kids that much older than me. They were more mature than me because they were older, and their bodies and brains were in different places than mine. Most of my daughter's friends are her age, maybe a little younger or not too much older. It's better for her. It would have been better for me to have friends my own age, and I would have had friends my age if I had listened when Uncle Nat and other family members were trying to keep me away from my older friends.

When I look back on it, though, I don't think I ever had more than few friends who were my age. I wanted to be with the older kids, so that's who I looked for and tried to hang around. I thought by hanging around with them, I'd be cool and more grown. I thought that hanging around with them made me as mature as they were, but I really wasn't. I was still 13 or 14 on the inside, I was just doing grown up things.

Like you already know, this caused me the kinds of problems you want to avoid.

Friends

My closest friends when I was in school were Tasha, Kiani and Ashley.   Of the three, Tasha was the friend who was in my life the longest, and who was probably my best friend.

Me and Tasha were tight--jam tight. We did everything together, and everything I had, she had, and every guy I dated, she dated his friend. We used to dress alike, act alike and be alike in every way we could. Tasha lived with her mom and her sister. Everyone said she was the pretty one. She had a cute little mixed look that the boys liked. She had the kind of freedom I wanted to have. She could stay out as long as she wanted to and sleep over at anyone's house she wanted to. I wanted to do that, too, but at the time I was living with Uncle Nat and Aunt Kris, and they wouldn't let me. They wouldn't let me have sleepovers either, so Tasha and I didn't get to do that, but just about everything else two friends could do, we did together.

We started hanging out in middle school and stayed tight all through school and beyond.

Even then, people were warning me about her.

"Tasha want to be like you," other friends and relatives said about her. "She always trying to copy off what you're doing and saying and wearing."

I did not see it like that. The way I saw it, we were just tight. Of course, Tasha and I wore the same clothes, talked alike, acted alike, and thought alike. It wasn't that she was copying me; it was that we were just friends like that. I thought it was completely normal for us to be so much the same. I thought that was just part of being real good friends.

Every now and then, Tasha would do something and I would wonder if we were the good friends I thought we were. Once, when she was dating a friend of Dream's named Bobby, she ended up going on a double date with Dream and another girl when Dream was supposed to be dating me. She didn't tell me.

I thought it was strange that she didn't say anything, especially knowing how I felt about Dream and all the drama he was putting me through with other girls. Maybe that's why she *didn't* tell me. She knew how much I was going through and she knew that the information would only hurt me.

That's what I told myself at the time.

She had her baby a couple of years after my daughter Reginae was born and had to get her daughter everything Reginae had. As Dream became more successful and shared his wealth with me and my daughter, I started to notice things I hadn't paid much attention to before.

Like how she was with money.

I never have been the sort of friend who kept score with money. If you're my friend, and you need something and I have it to give, I give it. I'm not like "You owe me that money" and I don't count every dollar I lay down versus how many you lay down. If we go out and you're short and I got something, I'll cover you and it's no problem. I figure you'll catch me the next time, or pick it up when I'm a little short. It'll even out because we're friends and that's what friends do.

Tasha wasn't like that, especially once Dream started really making money and everyone knew it. Tasha would give me $20 when we were out some place and I was running a little short, then come over the very next day at seven o'clock in the morning to demand her money back from Dream like I was some kind of deadbeat and she was the repo man.

"Where's my money at? Where's my money?"

I remember Dream turning to me with his mouth open in amazement.

"That's your *friend*?" he would grumble, reaching into his pocket.

As we got older, I noticed that while she always wanted to hang with me and was the first to accept an invitation to go out, her money never came out with her. She never wanted to pay for anything. She seemed to feel like I should cover everything with the money Dream gave me and that her only contribution should be to show up, even though she knew how much I hated to ask Dream for money and how much I had to go through just to get it.

"Opportunistic." That was the word people started using to describe her. "She's out for what she can get, and she's gonna try to get as much as you got."

I was warned. My older cousins told me over and over again, and they could see what I couldn't. You can't always go off what people tell you. You've got to go through it and learn it for yourself.

Finally, after years of friendship, I started to see it. I took her daughter to Disney World when I took Reginae. Of course, I paid all of the expenses and didn't ask her to contribute a dime, but she's never invited my daughter anywhere or out to do anything. Every year I send her and her daughter something nice for their birthdays, but when mine or Reginae's rolls around, not even a card.

Friends And Users

Don't get me wrong. I'm not boiling friendship down to who spends what and how much. I know not everyone has money to spend on gifts and stuff like that. But you do start to notice it when people are the first ones to want to hang when you're spending *your* money, and the first ones to complain when they have to spend their own. You start to notice it when people don't even offer to contribute to their own good time. You start to notice it when it seems like you're making all the effort in the friendship and the other person can't even remember to pick up the phone on your birthday.

The Mistake I Made That You Shouldn't

I let it go on longer than I probably should have because of how close we were when we were younger and the fact that our daughters were friends. The other mistake was that I didn't say anything about it, when I probably should have. I don't think she really knew how I was feeling and it might have made a difference if she'd known.

My friendship with Tasha taught me to watch out for one-sided friendships, and to avoid friends who only want me for what I have, who I know or what I can do for them. My friendship with Tasha taught me to be on the look-out for friends who try to copy everything I do.

For years, I had been talking about starting my own boutique. I love fashion, and I love beautiful clothes. I love helping other women find a look that sends a message or makes them feel sexy. It's been a dream of mine for a long time, and I've been talking about it long enough to make Tasha start thinking about opening a shop of her own.

I was trying to put my ideas together, find a location, get some investors and the like, and Tasha was doing the exact same thing. She found a great location and worked very hard on her store.

When her store opened, I went to support her. I spent money, and I told my friends. I found it strange that she never offered to help me get my store off the ground, share her expertise in retail, or even suggest that we go into business together, since we both had the same idea.

For Tasha, friendship was competitive, which I guess isn't the way I think good friends should be. After years of talking and planning, though, I did finally open my store, The Garb. It's got lots of stylish, fun, cool clothes that look great without costing designer money. When you're in New Orleans, you've got to stop by! Here's another example: When I found out that Dream was having a child with another girl, I was broken up. I had moved to Atlanta by then, and I was lonely and depressed anyway. The news that Dream had gotten another girl pregnant was really just too much for me. I didn't know anyone in Atlanta to talk to, so I called Tasha in New Orleans.

She shut me down.

I don't remember exactly what she said, but basically, she made it clear she didn't have time to listen to my problems. I was on my own.

Then, only a few months later, when she was going through something, I was on the phone with her for hours, talking it through. Our relationship had become really one-sided.

As for me and Tasha, I finally learned my lesson. In 2006, we took a trip to New York together to talk about our friendship. I tried to be really honest about what was bothering me and what had been happening between us, but Tasha never really said much about any of it. I had heard from some other friends that she had issues with me, too, but I guess she just didn't know how to communicate them to me. When we left New York, I knew that nothing had changed.

It was another lesson that you can't change people. You either accept them as they are and deal with them on that level, or you don't deal with them at all.

I finally just had to sit her down and say, "Tasha, we been friends a long time, but I think we've just grown apart. I don't think we're going to be chilling together as much in the future. "

She didn't like it. Not because it wasn't true, but because she could see that I had learned the definition of true friendship, and that competitiveness and one-sidedness don't have anything to do with real friendship.

Family

They say that crises bring out the best and the worst in people, and for my family, Hurricane Katrina was that crisis.

I was in Florida on vacation with Tasha and two other friends. We had gone to the VMA Awards that year and then stayed to have some fun in the sun. We had heard a little bit about a hurricane warning, but we weren't taking it too seriously. When you grow up living on the Gulf coast, there are hurricane warnings all the time. Most of them didn't amount to anything more serious than some rain and a little wind. I did pay a little more attention when I heard about the evacuation, but even then, I wasn't too worried. There had been several evacuations in recent years and they hadn't amounted to much more than some rain and a little wind, either.

So, as Hurricane Katrina blew in and destroyed whole sections of New Orleans, me and friends were mostly hanging out at the hotel pool or were on the beach having fun. I'm sorry to say it now because of all the terrible damage that the storm did and the number of people, some that I knew, who lost everything. At the time, we just didn't realize how bad it was going to be. We really hadn't been paying any attention to the news about it. It wasn't until we went to a restaurant and the waiter asked us, "Where you guys from?" that we really understood just what had happened and how bad it was.

"New Orleans," we said.

I had moved to Atlanta by then, but I still claim New Orleans as home because it's where I grew up and where my family is.

"Oh my God," the waiter said. "Are you here to escape the storm? Is your house okay?"

Friends And Users

That was the first we heard of how bad the situation was, and then when we turned on the news and we saw it, the vacation was over. We were all on the phones, trying to find family and friends, scared to death that one of our people had drowned or was trapped in their house or on their roof, waiting for help. I couldn't stand to watch all those people at the Convention Center and the Superdome, just sitting there in the heat without food or water. It was terrible.

We kept calling and calling. None of the phones were working. I started to get really worried and really scared.

We were driving ourselves crazy, worrying ourselves sick, and watching the news reports of one sad story after another. We couldn't get through to anyone because all the phone lines were down and even the cell phone towers had been damaged. Everything we saw on television made us even more nervous, and even more scared. We spent hours watching the news, crying and calling, until finally we realized we hadn't had any dinner and it was getting late.

We ended up in a club where O. J. Simpson was sitting at the bar, watching the news and talking about the storm.

"If y'all don't have a place to stay, you can come stay with me," he told us, which was nice of him, but in a way it made me feel worse. The fact that everyone was talking about it, that everyone was watching it, and that everyone realized how very, very bad it was made me want to jump on a plane or into a car and go there and find my family. It was an awful feeling, not

167
Antonia "Toya" Carter

knowing if they were alive or dead.

We kept calling. Finally we reached a few who evacuated before the storm hit. They were scattered all over Louisiana and Mississippi. Most were running out of money for hotels, or wearing out their welcome where they had landed. I told them all to come to me in Atlanta and left Miami, heading back home. I finally reached my Dad just as I pulled into my driveway. I was so relieved because other family had told me he had chosen not to evacuate. He had stayed in New Orleans throughout the storm. When I talked to him, he told me he was wading in water up to his thighs just to try to find fresh water and supplies. I told him to come to Atlanta, and he came after the storm was over on a Greyhound bus with a load of other evacuees.

My mom did evacuate and after a few nights on the road, she and all her family came to stay with me in Atlanta in my three-bedroom house.

There were probably about 30 of us crammed into what was suddenly a very small space. I made room for everyone, sleeping on floors and couches, cots and mats placed all over the house. What else could I do? I knew my people didn't have money for hotels. Almost all of their houses had been damaged to the point that they couldn't just go home and live in them. The water would have to go down and then repairs would be needed. It would take time.

Most of them were there for *months.*

It was incredibly stressful for everybody and unfortunately

some really ugly things got said.

My mom had a relapse and got high and said some really hurtful things that I don't know if I can ever forget, although I have already forgiven her. Stress and her addiction got to her, but even knowing that, I admit I was hurt. She doesn't remember what she said, but she's sorry for relapsing. For both of us, her battle against drugs continues.

One relative looked at my daughter and said, "You ugly like your father. Get out of this room." Of course, it was *my daughter's* room, but that didn't stop my guest from being rude and acting entitled.

"You married to a rapper? And you living in this little house? What's wrong with you? Why you ain't got more to show for yourself?" another grateful guest said.

I tried to put up with it. I tried to be helpful and patient. After all, most of them had lost their homes and everything in them. When the damage was all totaled up, my dad, my mom, my grandmother and even my own home in New Orleans were all destroyed. I lost my wedding pictures and all the pictures I took of Reginae when she was baby. All gone. If it hadn't been for one of my aunts who had saved a few of those pictures, I wouldn't have anything from those years.

I knew that my relatives had lost a lot, and I knew how bad they were feeling, but almost every day there were arguments, fussing, cussing and fighting. Almost every day my daughter was crying because of all the drama and the nastiness. I was never alone and no one seemed to feel bad that they were in my house, eating, sleeping, watching TV and using the bathrooms. Instead, I heard nothing but complaints.

I was very frustrated, but they had no respect.

Finally, it all came to a head and I just lost it. I don't like to fight with my family and I don't like to tell dirt on them, but I reached a point where I just didn't care. I didn't feel like they were respectful of me anymore and that made me lose a lot of respect for them, even though they were my elders.

"You can't come in here and do whatever. Cussing and acting ignorant. Treating this place like a hotel and my daughter like your servant. And this ain't a club, either, with loud music and drinks on the house," I told them. "We don't live like that. Either you act like you got sense and respect my house or we're gonna have to come up with something else."

Of course, they didn't like that. A few got offended and left and went to stay at a hotel. There are a few who don't have much to do with me since then. That's all right. In fact, it suits me fine. I'm past the point of tolerating disrespect just because we're related. I'm past the point of being used by anyone.

Finally, the FEMA vouchers and Red Cross aid cards and other relief started trickling in and most of the others left. I started taking the few who remained around Atlanta, trying to show them neighborhoods, trying to help them find a place--any place other than my house.

Finally, they were all gone. Almost all went back to New Orleans. Most of them aren't back in their homes, and they had to find other places to live, but they all went back. That's the thing about New Orleans. For all of us, it's home, no matter what.

The Mistake I Made That You Shouldn't

I'm a big believer in family, but I've learned that family will use you as much, or more, than anyone else. It was a mistake not to lay down the rules from the beginning and a mistake to tolerate as much nastiness and negativity as I did before saying something to put a stop to it.

Since I waited, I made it worse because by the time I finally said something, I wasn't just mad or annoyed. I was furious. Everything I said came out mean and hard, and by then I meant it, too. I'd had enough and they knew it.

These days, I don't have as much to do with my mother's family as I used to. I've learned by hard experience that when I'm around them, my feelings get hurt every time. It's not good for me, and it was really upsetting for my daughter, too. The time they spent in my house really helped me disconnect myself from my life in New Orleans. While I still visit and I still call it "home", I decided to sell my house there. I don't see myself going back there to live.

Sometimes you have to walk away from people who are all "take" and no "give."

It's a hard lesson to learn when you're talking about your own family, but it is what it is.

Jealous Friends

Have you ever had friends who were so jealous of you they couldn't stand it? Sometimes you can hear it in the things they say. Sometimes other people tell you things about them, things they've said about you behind your back, and you realize that while they're smiling in your face, they're thinking about sticking a knife in your back. Sometimes, the jealous friend is the type who never has anything good to say about anything. Everything is a criticism, and nothing is quite good enough. Just like user friends, you have to be careful when you deal with a friend who is jealous of you, or it can turn into a bad mess real fast.

Kiani was my friend, but she could never come to anything I was involved in. She didn't come to my wedding. She didn't come to my birthday parties.

"I don't want to hang on you like Tasha do. I'm a better friend than that," she used to say by way of explanation. It didn't make sense to me. If you're my friend and I invite you to celebrate with me, how does it prove you're "a better friend" if you don't show up?

Kiani seemed to think that if she held herself back a bit, she'd prove she wasn't a user.

I started noticing that when we talked, she spent a lot of time talking about my stuff and one-upping me. If I got a new

Friends And Users

purse, she'd tell me who she knew who got the bigger, more expensive size.

"Oh, you got the 2005," she'd say about my car. "My other friend got the 2006."

Mostly, she was very jealous of Tasha and me. If Tasha was hanging out with me, she'd make some excuse to make it sound like she was doing me a favor. "Oh, I don't want get in the middle of you two," she'd say. "But I'll be here when you need a *real* friend."

She must have tried a hundred different little comments to try to bust up Tasha and me. In the end, it was pretty easy to let her go because she never wanted to hang with me. She just wanted to talk about the people who did. These days, now that I'm doing all the things that I'm doing, she calls every now and then and says, "Don't forget your real friends."

For real? Now I'm creating my own brand, you want to hang out?

I don't think so.

Seriously, with fake friends you can't win for losing. You get talked about so bad no matter what you do, no matter what you say. I don't know how many times someone from my past has said, "You changed. You think you too good for us now" like I owe them something.

No baby, you wasn't with me *then*, and that's why you're not with me *now*.

I'm able to see that now, but when I was younger, I didn't understand the motives.

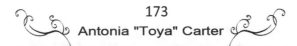

bar

173

Antonia "Toya" Carter

It's crazy, but I've had "friends" who were jealous of the way Dream provides for me and Reginae. One girl who I've known since high school also has a baby and a relationship with a guy in the music industry. She takes notes on what Dream does for me, and then uses those notes to try to get her man to do more. She'll come to my house and look at what I have, and then get on the phone to her baby's father.

"You know what Dream did for Toya?" I've heard her whine into the phone. "This is how a *real* boss treats his woman."

She actually took *pictures* of things I have!

Not good. Not at all.

The last time I saw that girl was at my birthday party a year or two ago. She came, she saw and I guess her jealous button got clicked. We don't speak at all anymore.

That's cool with me. I don't need friends like that.

I've also had friends who were jealous of the way I looked. Some of them want to compete with me about it, like it's some kind of "Who's the prettiest" contest. Some girls wanted to hang with me because they only hung out with pretty girls. You have to be pretty to be in some of the cliques. I've never much been into that. That's no way to choose your friends, based on what they look like. I've always wanted to be sure I was around people who loved me for the inside *and* the outside. And I'd never not be friends with someone just because of the way they looked.

I've actually had friends who'd say things like, "You can't come out with me tonight. I gotta find me somebody, and if you come they'll be looking at you and I won't get no attention."

For real?

Just because I like to look nice, you can't hang with me? Why don't you have confidence that you can meet someone regardless of who you're with and what they look like?

It's crazy.

No one wants people around them who are always criticizing or always trying to make them feel bad because of what they look like, what they've been lucky enough to get out of life, or who they fell in love with. People like to be around people who are proud of them, happy for them and want to see them do well.

I'm no exception. Sometimes it seems like some of my friends can't be happy for me. It's like they feel like I don't deserve what I've got, like I haven't worked hard for it, and it should have been them on TV, opening a store, getting married again, instead of me.

That's messed up.

A true friend would never do you like that, and I know, because I have some true friends.

True Friends

I met my friend Danielle shortly after I moved to Atlanta. She had just moved to the city, too, and we went to the same hair stylist. She's a few years older than I am, married and happy.

After I told her who my ex was, she nodded, but other than that, she never mentions him unless I do. She doesn't introduce me with him in the same sentence, like so many people do. From

Friends And Users

the beginning, she was like "That's my friend Toya." There's never been any of that "Dream's baby mama" stuff that only seemed to add another level of drama to so many of my friendships.

As I've said, even in Atlanta, I've met lots of girls who want to be my friend because of my past relationship. Comparing those girls with Danielle makes having a friend like her all the more special. She's been the one to help me plan parties and events. She's been the friend I tell my problems to. When I'm hurting, she cries with me, and when I'm feeling down and I'm struggling, she's the one to say "Let's plan a girl's day out!" and come up with something fun to do that will lift my spirits.

I can only hope I'm as good a friend to her as she's been to me.

The Mistake I Made That You Shouldn't

When you're young it's all about fun. You hear what you want to hear about the people you hang out with and the rest goes in one ear and out the other. As long as the person is fun, that's all that matters. You might have a lot of people around you, because a crowd makes it more fun to chill and kick it. What I've learned is that I only need a handful of really good friends and really loyal family members in order to be happy. Being able to tell a good friend from a bad one, and a fake friend from a real one, has been all about experience. I wouldn't listen when people told me about some of the people I had around me, so I had to learn the hard way. I had to get my feelings hurt, sometimes more than once. I had to get betrayed or backstabbed or lied about.

Now, I'm much better about seeing people's motives from the beginning. I've learned how to stay out those situations before they happen, just by being more cautious about who I call "friend." It's okay to have different friends for different reasons. There are friends that you hang with, friends you share career experiences with and friends who know all about every detail of your life. I've learned that it's okay to set limits on how much I tell certain friends, while with others, my life is an open book.

My circle isn't completely right and tight, but I'm a whole lot better at figuring out the game and shutting down the play. Back then I didn't know what I know now, but hopefully you can learn something from it and avoid some of the painful realizations that I had to discover the hard way.

Toya's Priceless Gem: Keep your circle of friends small and loyal. True friends don't care about what you've got, what you can do for them or what you look like. It's enough that you're you.

GOSSIP
AND THE TRUTH ♡

Antonia "Toya" Carter

Gossip And The Truth

Remember the saying: "Believe half of what you see and none of what you hear"?

If you've ever read anything about me on the Internet, please, please, please keep that old saying in mind!

It's crazy the stuff they put up on some of these blog sites about me, Dream, our daughter and our lives. Most of it is straight-up lies. If you believe the blogs, I've spent the past few years with a different guy every week, from football players, Eminem, to half of the city of Atlanta.

Not true.

Rumors and gossip, whether they are spread in conversations or through texting or on the Internet, are something that a lot of girls and young women have to deal with. Some people think it's cute to spread awful, nasty lies about the people they don't like, or the people that they are jealous of. Even at my daughter's school, there have been incidents where girls were texting and posting hurtful things about other girls, knowing that they were flat out lies. Gossip and rumors aren't cute at all. In fact, they can mess up people's whole lives, and the only thing I can say about people who spread that kind of trash about other people is that they must be truly, truly miserable.

I get talked about, and written about, plenty. I wanted to tell you about some of the stories and how I handle people who are lying about me. If you're going through it with some mean people who are telling lies about you, maybe these strategies will give you some inspiration to get through it.

Gossip And The Truth

Stretch Marks Make The News!

Once, I had a "wardrobe malfunction" (I wore a belly top!) and pictures of my stomach ended up all over the Internet. That's fine, except I have stretch marks on my stomach.

I got the stretch marks because I had a baby at a young age and gained a lot of weight. My skin stretched as I got bigger. Lots of women who've had children get stretch marks, but instead of pointing that out, people made all kinds of ugly remarks. It is what it is, people. I have stretch marks. Big deal. A lot of women have them, and I'm not ashamed of them.

For a while there, it felt like my stretch marks were the most important thing happening in the whole world. Everybody had to weigh in on how ugly they were, how dark they were, the whole nine.

Really?

This is breaking news? Toya Johnson Carter has stretch marks?

What about the war in Afghanistan? The record numbers of foreclosures and unemployment? What about natural disasters and corrupt politicians and all the problems we've got all over the world?

No. "Woman has stretch marks! More at 11!"

It seems like some people really love to find negative things to say. They don't want to hear anything positive. They don't want to know the story of how I donated the money for a girl from a less fortunate family to go to prom, from hair to shoes. They don't want to hear about the good I try to do in the community. They want to catch me doing something wrong, or acting silly or in my bathing suit, just so they can bash me!

What did I do about it?

I first heard about the stretch mark pictures on Twitter. I'm always on Twitter, both to promote the things I'm working on and to stay connected to people. I was getting Tweets from people telling me about the pictures being up on the blog sites. While I did go and check out what was being written and posted about me, I didn't respond to any of it. I didn't even reply to the tweets about it.

Why?

Because it's all a game. The bloggers need stories to drive traffic to their sites. Sometimes the stuff that they post isn't true, but without information, those folks don't get paid. So I try to look at it as them just doing a job, the best way they can. I try not to take any of it personally. Actually, when they *stop* talking about you is when you really have to worry!

You Weren't Invited to That Party

At Halloween a few years ago, me and my friends went to a costume party. After the party ended, we were looking for a place to go to keep having fun. We ended up in a club or something and the vibe was really fun. I probably had a glass of wine or maybe two. I was killing in this little sexy costume, and all of us were dressed up cute. We were taking turns dancing and wiggling, but really just for us girls. It wasn't like we were trying to entertain some men or working the pole or anything like that. I bet most girls have danced like I was dancing at that party. It was a great night and I really did have a good time, until the next morning when a video of us in our costumes acting wild and silly was posted all over the Internet.

Some people can take the fun out of everything.

I really didn't see what was wrong with it. We're all grown and it wasn't like we had our children with us. We might have been acting a little silly, but mostly we were dancing and talking and having fun. Our costumes were sexy, but it was Halloween. Why not? Costumes are part of the fun of the holiday. The things people had to say made it seem a whole lot worse than it was.

The only reason I saw any of it was because my friends called the next morning and they were like, "Toya, you gotta see it." So I went online and looked at it and I ended up reading a few of the ugly things people had posted about us. After I saw so much negativity, I was through with it. I shut the computer off and I didn't look at any more.

It seems like every time I go out, something pops up about it on the Internet and usually it's all wrong. They'll say I got a car and money, when I got a handbag, that Dream threw me a party when I threw it myself, that I got a special gift from one person, when it came from another one, and on and on. Sometimes it makes me feel that maybe I should just stop going out, stop having parties, and stop doing things with my friends.

Then I remember that when you stop doing the things you like to do because of what other people might say about it, THEY

WIN. I'm not going to do that. I'm not going to stop being me, and doing the things I like to do with the people I like to do them with because of what a bunch of haters might say!

Let them write whatever; I won't be reading it. I'm going to live my life and have fun!

Car Crash

People write things about my daughter, too. Once someone stole pictures of her in her cheerleading outfit and put them on a blog. Since she's a child, I was able to get the site to take the pictures down. I even made sure I got the pictures back, too. I might ignore pictures of myself and not comment on the lies at all, but she's just a little girl. There are safety issues and privacy issues with her. I'm not playing with that.

The worse thing of all the things that have ever been written or said about us by far was the awful rumor that Reginae had been killed in a car accident. The story started on one of those celebrity blog sites and then spread all over. It was all over Myspace.com and it even got picked up by MTV. It got so much play that finally Dream had to make a statement to let everyone know that it was a lie and that Reginae was fine.

I know the people at the site that originally posted this mess knew it was a lie. I know that. They did it to drive traffic to their website and to be the "first" to have some kind of celebrity information. They know that celebrities are easy targets for this stuff. They also know that once these kinds of rumors get started and spread and spread, people forget where they came from.

Gossip And The Truth

They are protected in the same way as girls who start rumors at school are--they just deny being the ones who started it and point the finger somewhere else.

Doing something like that to me or to Dream is one thing, but I have to wonder what kind of person would say such terrible things about a child. Our daughter isn't a celebrity. When she heard that the Internet was saying that she was dead, she was really, really upset. I don't think anyone would want to read that the whole world thought they were dead, when they're not. I wouldn't like it, and reading that awful mess about my daughter just made me really, really mad.

I don't know the person by name who started that lie, but I know one very important thing about them--they are lonely, sad and miserable. You know the saying "misery loves company?" It describes people who spread gossip and lies perfectly. They are miserable souls who can only find friends when they are talking trash about someone else.

I feel sorry for them.

How I Handle It

People ask me questions about things they've read on those blog sites all the time, and sometimes it seems like they really believe the things they've read. I don't get mad at them, but it does annoy me that these bloggers are out there writing things that aren't true. Not only does it mess up your image and your reputation, but if you get involved with it, it also steals your energy. If you've ever had someone start a story about you, and

Gossip And The Truth

spread it around your work or school or even your church, you know what I'm talking about. Sometimes people can start a story that can ruin your whole life. It can take years to recover what was lost because of a malicious lie.

As angry as these liars make you, you can't let them get to you. People can say what they want, but whatever they say, you know that's not *you*. They can say you are a freak, but if you know you aren't, then you are NOT a freak. They can say you've done anything they want to, but if you know you haven't, then you know the truth.

Tune it out. Pray for them. Brush it off. I know it's hard, but you can't let them know they are winning. If they know they're getting to you, they are going to keep doing it. If they see they aren't getting to you, then they'll stop.

Don't entertain it by fighting, either. Unless someone puts their hands on you, keep your fists down. Like I said about fighting over boys, it's just not worth it, and in the end it makes it worse. Nine times out of ten, the best thing to do to defeat haters is to keep smiling, keep striving and never let 'em see you sweat!

Toya's Priceless Gem: Don't spread gossip and rumors. Chances are good you're spreading a lie that could really mess up someone's life. If you're the one being talked about, hold your head up. Don't entertain it, and don't let it get you down. That's how liars win.

SELF ESTEEM AND BODY IMAGE ♡

Antonia "Toya" Carter

Self Esteem And Body Image

They say that nobody's perfect, though sometimes when I look at the video girls, I'm not sure that's really true. Looking at some of them makes me want to take any surgery there is, just to get a little bit closer to an ideal body! There are some really pretty girls in the world, but I guess that even they have something about themselves that they don't like. I know there are plenty of things I don't like about my looks, and sometimes, those flaws have made me pretty unhappy.

I'll admit it, my appearance is important to me. I pay attention to all of it--nails, skin, hair, makeup, figure, and clothes. I learned most of it from friends and watching other people, and I learned a few other things just by being embarrassed. There are a lot of things I wasn't taught growing up, like shaving and waxing. I can remember hanging out with my friends at school, and they would be talking about shaving, and I would be like "How come I didn't know I was supposed to do that?" It's definitely not cute for girls to have hair under their arms, but no one had taught me how to take care of myself when my body started changing. I learned most of what I know about taking care of my body and looking good from friends, and the rest from trying different looks and styles and seeing what worked for me.

All of us should try to be physically healthy, to have healthy habits and a good attitude. I think we should try to stay mentally and spiritually healthy, too. I'm not always the best about these things, but I do make efforts to take care of my body, to keep positive people around me, and to pray.

Antonia "Toya" Carter

If it helps inspire you to take better care of *you*, here's what I do to try to take good care of myself.

Body

Like I said, I think every girl and woman in America, and probably the whole world, has something she doesn't like about her body. For me, it's my stomach. I really hate it and I have to work hard to keep it as flat as it is. Being "thick" runs in my family. My aunts are all big women and it seems like their extra weight goes right around their stomachs. I'm not saying there's anything wrong with it. I've known lots of bigger women who always look good and who take really good care of themselves, but I'm not very tall and I don't think that's the best look for me. I'm actually really scared of getting too big. I'm not completely sure why. My best guess is that to me, getting big and getting old go together. I'm not looking forward to getting older either because I'm really scared of dying. I don't know why exactly. I believe in God. I'm just not quite ready to meet Him yet!

Maybe it's because I gained a lot of weight when I was pregnant with Reginae. And I mean *a lot*. Dream wasn't attracted to me at all while I was pregnant and while I still had my baby weight. I'm sure feeling unattractive while I was heavier is a part of the reason why I'm so uncomfortable when I gain weight. Take a look at the pictures of me from that time and you'll understand. I was really big after Reginae was born, and it wasn't like I just snapped back to being as small as I was before she was born. If you have had a baby, you know. It's crazy trying to get your body

Self Esteem And Body Image

back to the way it was before you were pregnant. I cut back on my eating and I got more exercise, but it still took a long time.

Even then, I was never the same.

Since I had a Caesarian section, there was a pouch of skin on my stomach that never went away no matter what I did. That pouch of fat and skin on my stomach bugged me so much, that finally, I had liposuction. I guess it helped, but in hindsight, I wish I hadn't done it because of the marks, the scars, it left on my body. My stomach is flatter, but now I have scars *and* stretch marks.

Oh well.

Just because you have lipo doesn't mean you get to stop exercising. I don't work out every day, but I do work out as often as I can. I do cardio and squats to keep my legs strong and get my heart rate up. I've been working on my arms (because I think they're kind of flabby) by using weight machines to get more definition. Reginae and I try to stay active by going on walks or bike rides together, fun things like that. I want to set a good example of fitness for her by doing things that are so much fun they don't feel like exercise, such as skating, dancing and bowling.

What I *don't* do is water. I'm afraid of water. Well, it's not really water that I'm afraid of, it's *drowning.* Although I'm working on overcoming that fear, I haven't completely beat it yet. I recently started taking swimming lessons, and while they've helped some, I'm still pretty scared. I think it may have started when I was kid, when my uncle used to throw me in the water. He meant it as fun, but it scared me. I wouldn't say I'm a fan of swimming and I don't see it as something I'll ever really like to do, but I don't want to be

Antonia "Toya" Carter

afraid of the water anymore and I don't want my daughter to be afraid of it. I'd like to be able to keep myself from drowning if it came to that. I don't think I'm quite there yet. I need some more lessons, but I hope I'll get there.

As important as exercise is, it's only part of taking care of your body. You have to try to eat right, too.

I'll be honest--eating healthy is hard for me. I like junk food of all kinds, and I grew up eating really heavy Southern foods, like macaroni and cheese and fried chicken. There weren't many vegetables on the plates I remember from my childhood, and the ones I do remember, I didn't like. It's only now that I'm older that I've begun to really like vegetables and make more of an effort to eat them every day. Even though I'm really trying hard to eat better, my favorite things are still ice cream, brownies and other sweets. I don't have much willpower. If they are around me, I'm probably going to eat them!

That's why I'm starting to buy different things and to think about what I'm eating differently. I'd rather have ice cream and brownies but I try to substitute fruit. I'd rather have bread, potatoes and butter, but I'm making room for more vegetables. Reginae hates them, but I know that fruits and vegetables are better for both us. I want to be around a long time, and I want her to have healthy habits as she gets older. She gives me a hard time about it, but whatever. She's a kid.

Even kids are struggling with obesity these days. When my daughter was around seven or eight years old, she started to get really chunky. Her friends were teasing her and saying things like "You need to diet" and other stuff. She was really upset by it. She didn't want to eat and her self-esteem was really suffering. It reminded me of when the kids at school used to tease me because I had a gap between my two front teeth. It wasn't until after I got braces and the gap was gone that I felt better about my smile. *Years* went by with me feeling like I had a messed up mouth, and kids picking on me and teasing me, first about the gap and then about the metal in my mouth.

Reginae was going through the same kind of thing, but instead of her teeth, it was her weight. Finally, I just sat her down and told her, "You're a growing girl. You are not fat. You don't need to diet. Don't let these kids get to you."

As she got older, Reginae's body changed and she outgrew that chunkiness. Unfortunately, like I did at that age, she's going to need some braces soon, so there might be some new teasing. As she gets older, Reginae gets better about ignoring the mean things some kids say. I tell her she's beautiful every day, and we work together to take care of ourselves.

I learned about make-up from watching people put it on. As I've said, I used to hang out with older friends and I'd watch what they did when they wanted to look really good. Though I like make-up, I don't wear much of it. I didn't wear it at all until two or three years ago. I'm not really a product junkie, and I don't buy a whole lot of different things for my hair or my skin, so there's no "miracle cream" that I swear by. In my daily life, I might just put on a little lip gloss and run out the door. Sometimes, I don't even do the lip gloss! When I'm doing TV interviews, though, I have to wear a lot of makeup. One of the only products I use faithfully is a makeup remover to make sure I get all of that stuff off!

It amazes me that the girls at Reginae's middle school are already wearing blush and mascara and lipstick. I think that's unnecessary. These girls are twelve years old! Some of them are so "grown" they even wear high heeled shoes! What are their mothers thinking? Poor Reginae--her mother won't even let her get the boots with the wedge heel. And makeup? No. You have a few more years, buddy. Sorry!

The thing that I do to take care of my skin is drink plenty of water. I drink water all day long, and not much else most days. I know it helps because my skin rarely breaks out.

The other thing I try to do to keep my skin healthy is get my full hours of sleep. I know some people have insomnia and can't sleep, but I'm lucky. I don't usually have any trouble falling asleep or staying asleep, unless there's a death in the family or of someone close to me. Death messes me up and keeps me awake. If someone close to me passes, I'm awake for weeks. I just can't sleep. I get scared. I start thinking all kinds of crazy stuff, worrying that I'll be next and that my time is up. It's a shame really. I pray every night, and I believe in God. I know that when it's my time, it's just going to be my time, but still, I'm afraid of dying. This is one of the reasons I'm really working hard to exercise, eat good, drink my water and sleep. I want to live a long, long life!

Self Esteem And Body Image

Mind

"Never let anyone dictate your happiness; find your peace within yourself." I don't know who said it, but it's a quote that I say to myself every single day. I memorized it a long time ago and whenever I'm feeling sad or down, or like I can't keep on going, I say it to myself over and over again. I have a lot of reasons to be happy, and I'm working every day to find greater peace inside myself. No one is responsible for my happiness but me!

I didn't always understand that.

I've always been afraid of failure. Most of my life I've been scared, terrified actually, to try new things because I didn't want to fail and look like a fool. Being scared of failing kept me from doing lots of things for a long time, even things I really wanted to do, like open a boutique or offer my services as a styling consultant. It was like there was this voice in my head saying "You can't do that" or "You don't have the right background to try that" or "Everyone's gonna laugh at you" or some other negative thought. I was miserable, scared and doing nothing much with my life other complaining and wishing.

Then, I had a long conversation with someone about how to beat back the fear of failure.

"Nothing beats failure but a try," they said to me.

Nothing beats failure but a try. I have forgotten who I had that conversation with, but I'm never going to forget the words. I live by them now. Whatever it is that you want to do, whatever it is that you hope to be, you can't get there if you don't try. You can't get there if you don't take the first step. No matter how scared you are, no matter what the fears are, you've got to give it a shot. Nothing beats failure but a try.

These days, I keep myself busy trying all kinds of things. I fail sometimes, and sometimes I don't reach the goals I set for myself, but I never feel as bad as I used to feel when I let self-doubt keep me from even trying. A lot of the time when I try something new, even if I fail, something good comes out of it, or the failure opens up a new possibility for me. So, even failure has turned out to be a learning experience that led to a new opportunity for me. Trying almost always leaves me with something good in the end.

Trying new things helps me to stay positive and it keeps me focused on what I can accomplish and what I can learn, instead of sitting around thinking about what I don't have. I know you can relate. When you have something new and exciting that you're working on, doing, or preparing for, you just feel better, right? So for me, keeping my mind healthy and my self-esteem high means always having something new and exciting to work on.

If you're feeling down, I'd really encourage you to seek out a new experience. Take the first step to a dream you've always had. Just try one small step, and when the fears or the negative thoughts start in your mind, tell them "Nothing beats failure but a try."

If you want to keep your mind healthy and positive, it also helps to surround yourself with positive people who will encourage you along the way, offer support and help you to see every new effort as a good step in a fresh direction. Some of the biggest mistakes I've made in my life have been made even worse by spending time with people who love negativity. I finally learned my lesson about that. Being around negative people just drags me down and I don't want that any more. I'm determined to keep my circle positive, and motivated. The more positive and motivated people I have in my life, the more energy I'm going to have to try new things and reach for higher goals.

If you're going to keep your mind healthy and positive, you need to make sure your circle is full of healthy and positive people. There's a saying that goes "Water seeks its own level" and it means that things that are alike find their way to each other. You want to make sure that your friends are positive people? First take a hard look at yourself. Are you a positive person? Are you working on making yourself better? Are you trying new things and making your dreams come true? If you aren't, don't worry about finding new friends first. Take care of your own house, and the friendships will take care of themselves. You'll find, like I did, that when you change, your friends change. The old negative relationships end up fading away one at a time.

Spirit

When I was growing up in New Orleans, I used to go to church almost every week. I was raised a Catholic and when I was a child my relatives would take me to Mass on Sundays. The older I got, the more I realized that I didn't really understand the religion at all. Nothing against Catholics or the Catholic faith, but I guess I didn't get enough education about the religion when I was younger and I felt disconnected in the services. By the time Reginae was born, I really needed my faith more than ever, but I was looking for a different way to celebrate it. I converted and became a Baptist in my late teens.

When I was still living in New Orleans, I would take my daughter and my little brother (he was living with me by then) to the Baptist church every Sunday. When Dream was in town, I would try to get him to go, too. Sometimes that worked, but most of the time, it didn't.

Later, when I moved to Atlanta, I started going to a different Baptist church, a mega church led by a very, very well-known minister. I stopped going there when I started to feel that the congregation worshipped the pastor, and not God. It really bothered me that they didn't seem to know the difference! It wasn't just that. It was also that being in a crowd of 20,000 people made me feel like I was at a concert, and not like I was in church. Once again, I decided I needed a change.

I started looking around for another church, a smaller one, and a place that could become my church home. I tried a bunch of churches, but I never found what I was looking for, so eventually I stopped looking. However, I didn't stop praying and I've never stopped thanking and praising God.

I pray every night before I go to bed, but it's more than

Self Esteem And Body Image

that. I pray all the time. I'll be my car, having conversations with God. I ask for guidance and help. I ask for wisdom and courage. I ask for more faith. I ask for forgiveness. Mostly, I thank Him. I thank Him for my many, many blessings. I thank Him for waking me up to another day. I thank Him for my family and good friends and for all the positive people in my life who motivate me to do better. I thank Him for everything. Sometimes, when I'm driving around I just speak whatever's on my heart and thank Him and praise Him. I'm blessed. I've been blessed since I was kid. When I'm just riding along running errands or whatever, I'm praying. I'll just be feeling so good and grateful that I just have to start thanking Him. If it weren't for God, I don't know where I would be, or what my life would look like. I'm not just talking about material things. I'm talking about my good health, and my daughter's good health. I'm talking about having all my senses. I'm talking about having a new man, my love, beside me. I thank God for bringing someone like him into my life and for all the things that have nothing to do with money or possessions that make life so wonderful.

I am truly, truly, blessed.

I used to feel like you couldn't have it all. I thought you couldn't be both successful and happy. I didn't think you could have both money and true love. I tried to make the best of what was missing in my life. I had married a rapper and had an extravagant lifestyle, and I wasn't happy. I thought that was just the way it had to be--you're either happy in love and struggling financially, or you have it made financially, but the love is lacking.

I was wrong.

You *can* have it all. I know because I feel like I really do have it all. I have my own nice things, I have good man who I love and who loves me, and I have a healthy, talented daughter. I guess it's all about the timing, and when God is ready for you to have those things, you have those things.

Or maybe, when your mind is ready to really receive those things, and to accept them with gratitude, God provides them.

Even if all of the good things in my life were taken away tomorrow, I would still pray and still thank God. I believe absolutely that He is in control of my life, and this helps me to feel spiritually healthy and spiritually at peace. Praying reminds me that not everything is up to me, and I have to accept that in the end, God is the master and I am the servant. Knowing that His Will is done eliminates a lot of the stress in life, and stress isn't healthy at all.

The Mistake I Made That You Shouldn't

As I've said, appearance is important to me. I like to look good, and I try hard to stay in shape. I regret that I let the video girl image get me feeling so bad about myself that I had the liposuction. I wouldn't do that again. It's really easy to get sucked into trying to look like someone else instead of celebrating and taking care of the body that you have *right now.*

Don't make that mistake. The best thing you can do is continue to make good, healthy choices that really add up, like

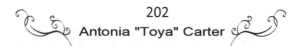

eating fruits and vegetables, drinking lots of water, trying to get some kind of exercise every day and getting your full sleep. Fill your life with positive people and new experiences, and don't be afraid to fail, like I was. Also, don't forget to thank God for everything in your life. Counting your blessings makes you appreciate them that much more.

Toya's Priceless Gem: Whatever your size or shape, find ways to take care of your body, mind and spirit. Even small changes can add up to a big difference!

TRUST AND REAL LOVE♡

Trust And Real Love

They say you can't really love someone if you don't trust them, and I believe it. I've learned the hard way that you can say you love someone and you can have a lot of deep feelings for them, but if you're worrying about what he's doing and who he's with all the time, then you don't really trust him. If you don't trust him, the love you have isn't true. Real love and real trust go hand in hand.

Trusting people isn't easy, especially if you've had your heart broken into tiny pieces like I have. Betrayal makes you feel like the whole world is full of liars, cheaters and people out to do you harm. Betrayal makes you doubt that anyone is really what they say they are, or that they'll do what you hope they'll do. Your guard goes up real high, so high that hardly anyone can get past it, and that's the way you want it. I know I felt like I needed to keep my guard up after my marriage ended. It felt like the only way to take care of myself was to raise my guard and never, ever let it down again.

Don't get me wrong--being cautious isn't always a bad thing, especially when it comes to men. There are dangerous guys out there, there are guys who just want to play, and there are guys who are users. It's just smart to hesitate and to step back a bit and make sure everything is cool before you decide to start kicking it with someone. If you're really looking for someone to share your life with, at some point you have to find a way to balance being cautious with being open enough to find love again.

For the longest time, I knew I wanted to be in love again, but I was afraid. I was afraid that I'd fall deeply in love with

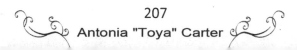

someone who might take advantage of my feelings and treat me bad. I was afraid I'd be back on that painful roller coaster of loving and fighting and loving and breaking up. I was afraid I'd be the one waiting and wondering again, while he moved from girl to girl.

When I thought about all the negative things that might happen if I got serious in a new relationship, it seemed easier to just leave the whole business alone. You've heard that saying "I can do bad by myself?" It was sort of like the opposite of that for me. It wasn't that I was doing bad. It was that I was doing *good*, putting my life together step by step, and finding a place where I was truly happy with myself and what was going on around me. I was afraid that falling in love again would only mess it all up.

I wanted love and I didn't. I wanted a new relationship, and I didn't.

You feel me? Have you ever been in that situation where you both want something and you don't want it, and you don't know what to do about it? I don't think I understood at the time that my fears about love were the same things as my fears about trust. I definitely didn't realize that the person I most needed to trust was myself. Trusting the guy wasn't nearly as important as learning to trust myself to pick the right one.

I couldn't love and trust anyone until I learned to love and trust myself more. I needed to believe in my own choices. I needed to believe that I could pick the right kind of man for the next part of my life. I needed to become more sure that I could make the right decisions for myself and my daughter before I brought a man who might become her stepfather into our lives.

Trust And Real Love

I didn't have a plan for doing this, but, looking back, I see how it happened. Maybe this story can give you some clues for finding a deeper love and trust in yourself, too.

Learning to Trust Me

I think I first started to learn to trust myself by accident. It started when Dream and I were married and the relationship wasn't working. I was sick and tired of being sick and tired. I had swallowed down so much anger, and I had put up with so much that I just couldn't take it anymore. Something in me just exploded. I was pissed off about so many things--my relationship, the way people were talking about me, and the lack of support I felt from family and friends. It was all pressing down on me like a heavy weight. It wasn't so much that I thought to myself, "I'm just gonna trust my feelings on this one." It was more like, "I'm sick of this crap and I just can't take anymore."

I felt like whatever I did or said next, things couldn't get any worse. Dream and I were over and I hated living in his shadow. If one more person introduced me as "Dream's wife" or "Dream's baby mama", I was afraid I'd punch them out and end up in jail for assault. I couldn't live in New Orleans anymore where everyone knew me for that one relationship. I felt like no one cared about me for me, Toya. I finally decided, "To hell with what anybody else thinks. I have to get out of here!"

It was almost like desperation, or self-preservation. I felt like I had to get out or I would go crazy. I felt like I had to get out or I might die.

Making that single, desperate decision was when things started to change for me. Like I said, I wasn't thinking "Gee, Toya, you need to trust yourself more." It wasn't like that. What I felt was *raw*. It came not from my mind, but from a place deep in my heart. When I started thinking and feeling that way, that I would just go crazy if I didn't do something different, was when I started making decisions just for me. It was when I finally stopped worrying about other people and doing what I felt like *I* needed to do, and trusting that whatever happened, it would be okay. Making that shift was when I started to feel better about myself, my life and my place in the world.

Sometimes, after you've been through a lot of mess, it's easier to take the kinds of chances that can change your life. At least that was true for me. All the drama I had been through made me feel like I had to do something, anything, to bring a change. If you're in a similar situation, use your feelings of being pissed off or fed up to take you to your next destination, whether that destination is a new job, or a new school or, like me, a new city.

I try to remember that feeling that I had in my heart when I have to make decisions now. I try to find that feeling because it brought me in touch with *me*, with the real Toya and what I really wanted. Your heart always speaks to you and if you can turn off what other people are saying and listen to it, you're on the way to trusting yourself.

Too many of us don't trust ourselves at all. We're always going to other people to help us make our choices. We've got to call sixteen friends just to decide if we want to go out to dinner or how to spend our own money. I know you know some girls who talk over every single thing with their friends. Everything. You might even be that girl. Or maybe you're not quite *that* bad, but when it comes to the big decisions in your life, you find yourself calling other people and looking for guidance. I know I used to be a lot more like that than I am now. I felt like I didn't know enough to trust my own feelings. As I got older, I realized that, while there are plenty of things I don't know (and there isn't anything wrong with asking people who are more knowledgeable for information), the decisions are still mine. I still might reach out for help or even advice from people who have had more experience. At this point in my life though, I know that the opinions of others don't have to rule my life. If what others say doesn't feel right or if I don't have peace about it, I don't do it.

Sometimes, this makes people mad, and while I don't like hurting people's feelings, there are times when it can't be helped.

When Tiny and I first started thinking about doing a TV show, we lost a friend, but the decision wasn't about intentionally hurting anyone. It was about trusting what we both felt in our hearts.

Originally, we wanted to do a talk show. I still think that would be fun. There are lots of interesting topics out there, and I think we could do something that everyone could learn from. Me, Tiny and another friend put something together and approached James DuBose of DuBose Entertainment about it. Our idea was that we could do something like *The View* with the three of us

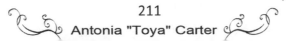

discussing various topics and having on guests, too.

The folks at DuBose Entertainment had a different idea, a reality show for BET. I thought it was interesting, but I wasn't ready to decide. BET was just one of the networks we were talking to and while it was an interesting idea, we wanted to see if maybe another network might buy our talk show idea.   We went from meeting to meeting with our talk show idea, but most of the other networks weren't interested at all. When we were done making our pitch, the only other interest came from MTV, but they didn't like the talk show idea either. Instead, they wanted to do a reality show, too. Their idea was something that focused more the men the three of us had been involved with, particularly on Tiny's man, who had a movie coming out, and with us ladies as simply background.

Well, you know for me that was a "no." By then I'd come to the point where I knew that whatever I did, it had to be as *me*, Toya. Not as the ex-anything of anybody. I was done with that.

We hoped that having MTV put something on the table would give us some leverage with DuBose Entertainment and BET to try to do our original talk show idea. It didn't work the way we planned. They still wanted to do a reality show or no show at all.

Well, Tiny and I were like, "Okay." We thought we might shop our idea around a little bit more later and see if things had changed. While we had own ideas about it, we weren't really pressed or stressed about it. I guess we both had a feeling down deep that it would work out the way it was meant to. We had trust in ourselves, trust in our idea, and trust in God. We were cool with BET having a different idea, but we were just going to think about it a while longer.

It wasn't a big deal.

My other friend freaked out. She went all crazy on the guy, calling him out of his name and throwing her finger in his face. It was not pretty, not at all. When we left out of that meeting, I felt like a bridge had been burned forever.

Still, I was okay with it. I was disappointed that the talk show idea hadn't found a home and embarrassed that someone I was so closely associated with had showed her butt so badly, but something inside me trusted that it would all work out.

Sometime later, DuBose Entertainment and BET called again to say that they wanted to move forward with a reality show concept built around Tiny and me, and without the other girl. I had a moment when I was like "what about my friend" but it only lasted a moment. There was a time when I might have passed up that opportunity if my girl wasn't included, but I felt inside me that this time taking the show was the right thing to do *for me*. I didn't think the girl who was cut out of the cast would be mad about it. I mean, what did she think was going to happen after she went in there and cussed and screamed and carried on? That everyone would just forgive and forget?

Forgive, maybe, but forget? Would *you* forget someone coming into your office and disrespecting you? Would that be someone *you* wanted to work with in the future?

If I had done that, the only person I would have had to

be mad at would have been myself, for real. This girl was mad at everybody. She then proceeded to go on the Internet and try to bash everybody.

One of the things that experience taught me, though, is that sometimes when you just let go and trust that everything is going to work out, everything does. I had one clear boundary for the whole thing--that whatever we did was about us girls and not about the men we had been involved with. Other than that, I was cool with whatever ended up working out. Sometimes, when you stop trying so hard to "make something happen" and just have some faith, God will do better by you than anything you could have dreamed up on your own. I know that's been true for me.

The Mistake I Made That You Shouldn't

I spent a lot of years worrying about what other people thought. I was afraid to trust myself until I finally just got fed up. When I finally just said, "enough!" my situation got better. I finally started doing what I wanted to do, without worrying about what anyone else thought about it. I finally started to focus on just me. I started to look for that real, raw feeling down in my heart and using it as my guide. That was the beginning of learning to trust myself, and I wish I'd done it sooner.

No matter what you do, someone's always going to be mad about it, so it's important to realize that in the end, you have to trust yourself enough to do what's right for you.

Don't wait until you're about to explode before you trust yourself. Don't make my mistake.

Trust And Real Love

Loving Me

Everyone always says the greatest love is learning to love yourself. Actually it's the hardest thing in the world to do, especially when everything seems to be going wrong and people are leaving you right and left. It sometimes seemed to me that I had done so many things wrong that there wasn't much about me that anyone could love. It also seemed like so many people had walked away from me at one point or the other that there must be something unlovable about me.

Probably every one reading these words has felt this way--unloved and unlovable. The truth is, when you're feeling like this, people can talk about "loving yourself" all they want to, but it doesn't change much. When you're feeling bad about yourself, it's not always easy to find anything about yourself that's worth loving.

At my lowest points, when I was so in love in Dream and he wasn't in love with me anymore, or when there were so many haters talking bad about me and it was hard to find true friends, or when Aunt Edwina died and I realized how alone I was in the world, I didn't love myself. I didn't even *like* myself. Since I didn't like myself, I sometimes made decisions that ended up hurting me.

It wasn't until I left New Orleans and moved to Atlanta that I really started to try and figure myself out. Who was I really? If I wasn't Dream's girl, or my mother's daughter, who was I? What did I want to do? What did I have to offer the world, other than being a rapper's ex?

For a while, those were really hard questions. I knew what I *liked* to do—fashion, hair, and helping other people achieve a look that made them feel beautiful and confident, but I didn't have the confidence to believe that anyone would seek me out for that help. I didn't even know how to go about putting myself out there as someone with those skills. I could hear people laughing at me: "Toya thinks she's a stylist, now? She must be tripping!"

Actually, I *was* tripping. I was tripping because I didn't think I was good at anything. I had failed at everything from my high school exit exam to my marriage. How could I think I could succeed in such a competitive industry as fashion styling?

The only *real* thing I was absolutely sure I was good at was being a mother.

I am proud to say that I'm a good mother.

I've made some mistakes, but for the most part, I've done pretty good. I can tell by the relationship Reginae and I have. She knows she can talk to me about everything and anything, and she does. She knows I love her, and I tell her every single day. She knows I'm proud of her. She knows there are limits and that while she's still a child, I will do everything I can, and give everything I have, to protect her and keep her safe. She knows about the

Trust And Real Love

serious mistakes I made and that, even though I've been able to make lemonade out of the lemons, it wouldn't be the smartest choice for her to follow in my footsteps.

I knew I liked fashion and I knew I was a good mother, and as I became more comfortable in Atlanta and started meeting more and more people, I began to realize another thing that I was good at--I'm a good and loyal friend.

It's true. I started meeting people and making friends. Sometimes I met them at events that I was invited to, and sometimes it was just doing errands, or at the hair salon. People seemed comfortable with me, and they told me their stories. I shared with them some of the things I'd been through.

I began to see myself as family-oriented and realized that I had really tried to help my relatives. Sometimes that got me into trouble. I tried too hard to please people who didn't have my best interests at heart, but the spirit of it was a good thing.

I began to see myself as a good person. I was a person who had made some mistakes, and I was a person who had weaknesses and faults, but I was a good person, a person I liked, and a person who tried hard and was honest, loyal and real.

Two years ago, I had the words "I love me" tattooed on my finger. It was my reminder to myself to treat myself like I was as priceless as my name. It was my reminder that I was a gem, and that the time for making decisions for my life that were wrapped up in what other people thought or wanted was over.

I had finally decided to make my life about *me.*

It hasn't been easy, but little by little, I've started to

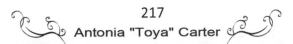

recognize more and more of my good qualities. I've started to feel better about myself. Feeling better about myself has helped me to reach for new opportunities. Reaching for new opportunities has helped me to see that I was capable of so much more than I thought I was when I was sitting in my house in New Orleans, wondering why Dream didn't love me anymore. I started to make friends who saw all my good qualities. They've praised them in me. It's been like a snowball--the more confident I felt, the more new things I tried. The more new things I tried, the more new people I met. The more new people I met, the more new things I learned. The more new things I learned, the more I liked myself. The more I liked myself, the more confident I felt. The more confident I felt, the more new things I was willing to try.

I made new goals for myself. One of them was to try to do more fashion styling and to hold fashion shows. Another was to open a boutique. I got the opportunity to try styling on *Tiny and Toya*, and I know I'm going to be doing more of it. I'll be hosting more fashion shows in the community at my boutique, The Garb.

I'm really, really proud of the store because it's something I've wanted to do for the longest time, and it's something I'm doing 100% on my own. For years, I tried to open the store, but I thought I needed either the financial backing or assistance from my ex. One thing and then another seem to keep it from ever happening.

Finally, The Garb is open on Magazine Street in New Orleans, and I did it all myself. In addition to offering high-style at recession prices, it even has a section that includes a little bit from my own wardrobe called "Toya's Closet" where you can buy dresses I wore on the red carpet or outfits that I've been photographed in.

I'm proud of it, and I'm proud of me.

The other really big goal that I set for myself was to write this book, and as you can see, I've done that, too. I'm proud of it, and I'm proud of me. Not in a conceited way, but because I set a goal for myself and I accomplished it.

Finally, I really started to see myself as loving and lovable, and once I started to see myself as loving and lovable, love came to me.

The Mistake I Made That You Shouldn't

For a long time I believed that I was only lovable when someone was in love with me, or when I felt the love coming to me from others. I wish I'd realized sooner that being in a relationship isn't what makes you lovable. Instead, it's what you have in your heart, what you give to other people and how you use all the qualities and abilities that you have that are gifts from God.

I was lovable even when no one loved me, and now I know that. By exploring new things and new places, I've discovered things about myself that I like and strengths I didn't know I had. I've learned to love myself for who I am, and loving myself has made it easier for me to love others.

Toya's Priceless Gem: Starting to love yourself means looking at the things you're good at, at the qualities you're proud of and the good you do for other people in the world. Every time you find things you like about yourself, you come closer to realizing that you are a priceless gem, and to learning to love yourself for exactly who you are!

Loving and Trusting Others

I've been hurt enough times in relationships to be real suspicious about men. When I meet a new guy, I hesitate. Lots of things run through my mind: What's his motive? Is he a player? Is he looking to get famous or to use me? Is he dangerous? My life has given me reason to be suspicious.

I've had plenty of dealings with people whose motives with me weren't good. I've had my share of bad experiences with men who just wanted to be with all the girls and who weren't interested in building anything serious with just me.

I've met plenty of guys who, as soon as they found out a little about me, wanted to use me to get famous. They wanted me to hook them up with the people I'm associated with, but after that, they weren't really interested in getting to know me.

After being followed by a stalker fan, I have learned to be cautious about the people I meet casually in public. I couldn't take the chance that someone who saw me on TV and claimed to "love me" might get too close to me or my daughter.

Even before the show, I sometimes met guys who weren't

Trust And Real Love

quite right, you know what I'm saying? Sometimes you can tell when you first meet them, but sometimes, it takes a minute for you to realize it. That's how it was when I met a guy I'll call "Sam" when I first moved to Atlanta.

At first everything was great. I liked Sam and he seemed nice. Pretty quickly I could tell he was more into me than I was into him. He really liked me, and after only a couple months of pretty casual hanging out together, he started talking about getting married. We'd be driving around the city together, and he'd be pointing at houses.

"You like that one, Toya?" he'd ask. "I'm gonna buy it for you."

I thought that was a little strange. I hadn't known him long enough to even start thinking about a serious relationship, and he was already talking about settling down?

It got worse.

I don't know if you would call it stalking, but he kept popping up on me everywhere I went. If I went to visit a friend, he'd be driving in the neighborhood, or even stop by her house. If I went to the grocery store or to run some errands, there he was. It made me really uncomfortable. I felt like he was checking up on me or something, trying to make sure I was where I said I was. That's bad, even if you are married to each other, because if you don't have trust, then you don't have a relationship. We didn't have it like that. We weren't married. We weren't even boyfriend and girlfriend. We'd just been on a few dates, and that was it.

This went on for a couple of weeks before I got sick of it. I

broke it off with Sam and I told him why. I let him know that I just didn't like the possessive vibe he was sending out. He went crazy. Somehow he got his hands on some pictures my friends had taken of me and he put them all over the Internet along with my phone number. "She's a freak!" he wrote on this website, detailing all kinds of nasty stuff I would do to them if they'd call the number. It was really sick.

Sam also caused me problems at home, too. My little brother was living with me then, and Sam convinced him that they were friends. So my brother was telling him where I was and taking his side in my house! I had a serious talk about loyalty with my brother, which he really didn't like. He got mad and left me to go back to other relatives in New Orleans. It took a while to sort all that out and for my brother to understand how Sam had been using him to try to force me to continue dating him.

At the lowest moments of my experience with Sam, I was afraid to stay in my own home. I don't know what would have happened if he hadn't decided to go back to New Orleans (he was from there, too).

He went back, and ended up getting killed. I guess he ran into some trouble down there. I really don't know the story, but I heard that someone shot him. By then, I had already decided--no more dating for me. None. I went on a loooong break from men.

It wasn't just the experience with Sam. My dear friend Shawnte's murder a little while later really put the lock on it for me. Some of the things she went through were things I had avoided just by luck with Sam. I felt like I had every reason to worry about violent and abusive men. The way she died shook me up so badly that for a long time I didn't take any chances with anyone. In every man's face I saw the potential for harm hiding just beneath his smile. I wouldn't let my guard down to any of them because of this for a long time after her death. I was just too scared. I didn't want her fate to become my own.

Little by little, I started to realize that my fears were cutting me off from adding the possibility of a happy relationship to my life. I knew I had to be cautious or I'd make the same mistakes I had in the past, and get swept up in a relationship with someone who could never really be serious about me. I knew I had to be cautious or I might become a victim of someone who claimed to love me, but was actually unstable. While I'll never forget the lessons of Shawnte's death, I don't want to live my life being so suspicious that love can't find me. Some men are abusive, but not all of them are. I had to trust that I'd learned something from Shawnte's experience and at the first sign of something "off", back out of the relationship and move on.

I wanted a man in my life, but I wasn't feeling desperate about it. I'm not one of these women who loudly proclaim they "don't need a man." It's true, I don't *need* a man, but I do *want* someone to share my life with me, and that's just the truth.

I met my guy, Memphitz, a couple of years ago at T-Pain's BET Awards after-party. I usually don't date guys I meet in a club because when you meet a guy in a club, you know something really important about him—that he clubs. Guys that go to clubs to hang tend to be boys, still playing. They haven't grown up.

They haven't become men who are interested in something *real*.

The after-party had a club feeling to it, but because it was at a beautiful private home in Los Angeles, I made an exception to my usual rule about men I meet in that atmosphere. We talked. It was nice. He was a different kind of guy than the guys I usually meet. I found him interesting, and at the end of the evening, I broke my other rule and gave him my number.

We hung out when we could. We were both busy and had a lot going on in our lives, so it wasn't like dating or any big love affair at first. He had a house in Atlanta, but spent a good deal of his time in New York. When he was in Atlanta, he'd call and we'd chill around the city, getting to know each other.

We started out more as friends than anything else. He had a situation and I had a situation and neither of us was free, so it really couldn't have been much more than friendship. I was involved with a player from the Buffalo Bills, and he had a girlfriend. We talked about those relationships. We tried to give each other advice. It was like having a good friend from the opposite sex to help give you another point of view.

I invited Memphitz to my birthday party and he brought me a present--a pink gun.

I was still dating the player, but things hadn't been good in a bit and I was starting to feel that he wasn't the right guy for me. In one of our many conversations, I'd told Memphitz that I wanted a little gun. I wanted to learn to shoot for protection. After the incident with the fan who tried to follow me home, I was rattled. I was a woman alone with a young daughter. I don't have security,

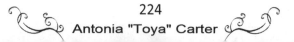

and I don't have guards. I wanted a gun--a pink one. (Hey, I'm a girl!) I'm not trigger happy and I'd hope to never, ever use it, but I knew it would ease my mind to have it.

Here was Memphitz with a pink gun in a pretty little box for my birthday.

I was really touched. It was sweet that he'd remembered, and it made me see him in a different light. He was really paying attention to what I was saying, and he really wanted to see me happy. Most of the guys I'd hung out with only paid attention to what made them happy. They rarely gave the women in their lives much thought at all.

It was a real light-bulb moment for me.

Memphitz had proved to me he was different from most other guys. We were still just friends, but the thoughtfulness of his present kept coming to my mind again and again.

Of course, the player didn't like Memphitz or his present. He felt disrespected because someone else had shown more thoughtfulness toward me than he had. I didn't care. I was ready to break up anyway. I wasn't going to let someone who wasn't really feeling me tell me to cut off a friend who genuinely cared for me.

No way.

Meanwhile, my friendship with Memphitz continued to grow. When the time was right for both of us, we finally took our three and half year friendship to the next level. We got engaged and are planning to marry soon.

I'm happy.

I can tell you, it's wonderful to be in love again. I feel very secure about this relationship because it grew so slowly. We really know each other and neither one of us was swept away in a big fairy tale kind of romance. We love each other because we're friends first, and lovers second. He's good to my daughter. He treats her like one of his own kids. My daughter loves him and is happy, too.

I'm not expecting happily ever after, but I do expect we'll work together to build a good life.

I wish the same for you.

Toya's Priceless Gem: When you really love and trust yourself, you won't accept less than real love and trust in your relationships. If your relationships aren't working, he's only half the problem. The other half is you, and you're the one you need to love the most.

Afterwords

Since we started doing *Tiny and Toya*, people have been asking me:

"When you gonna write that book, Toya?"

"Where can I get your book?"

I knew I wanted to write a book, but it seemed like a pretty big undertaking. Even though I've been through some stuff in my life, stuff that people seemed to be able to relate to, I didn't want to just talk about myself. I wanted to try to write something that meant something to young girls and women out there who might be going through some of the same things, and feeling some of the same feelings that I felt.

I hope I've been able to do that because even if your name isn't "Antonia", you ARE priceless. If anybody says otherwise, you send 'em to me.

Love,

Toya

Diary

Diary

Diary

Diary

Diary

Diary

Special Thanks and Acknowledgements

Before I thank anyone else for all of their help and assistance in getting this book written, I want to thank God. Without Him giving me the experiences I've had and giving me the ideas He did, this book would not have been possible.

Secondly, I have to thank my daughter, Reginae. You are my princess, my reason for being, and my everything. Thank you for being you and always know that I love you. I owe many thanks to my family. I thank my mom and dad for giving me life and my Aunt Edwina and my Uncle Frank for raising me to be the strong woman that I am today and for constantly pushing me to do better. My sincere thanks go to Nathaniel Holden for always being my rock, and for being the consistent man in my life throughout the years. Even though he had his own family, he always made room for me and he was always there, trying to steer me toward the right, even when I wanted to go left. I also am grateful to his wife, Kristalyn Holden, for always being an ear for me and always listening and offering support.

Cheryl Washington, I thank you for being for such a good big sister/cousin to me. Then there's Kathy Williams, Frank Holden, Jr., and all of the Holden family for accepting me like a little sister and always looking out for me. Thanks go to all of my brothers and sisters—we've lost a lot of time, but all of you have embraced the whole situation and I'm looking forward to a bright future. Many thanks also go to Jacida Carter, Dwayne Carter and the Carter family for their love and support through the years. I also want to thank my grandmother, Helen, for teaching me the importance of having tough skin, and to my grand-fathers, Tillman and George, and my other grandmother, Jackie, for connecting me to my history.

Thanks and love to my friend, Danielle, for showing me what true friendship is all about. You truly are the best. My friend, Lydia, has been extremely helpful and, of course, I can't forget my "Glam Squad," LaTasha Wright and Rikya Taylor, who make sure that I always have the right look for every event and occasion.

I also want to thank James Dubose, my new brother, for believing in me when nobody else did. My love and thanks to Tiny for being such a good friend, and to all of the fans for watching *Tiny and Toya* and making it such a success. My attorney, Uwanda Carter, was extremely helpful too in seeing this project through to completion, as well as all of the people at Farrah Gray Publishing, especially Dr. Farrah Gray, Shannon Leon and Karyn Folan for all of their help with getting this project out of my head, onto paper and into bookstores.

And last, but not least, thanks to Mickey Wright, Jr. for being the love of my life, and for understanding me and accepting my daughter as his own. I love you dearly.